THE GROWTH OF
AMERICAN ENGLISH

William A. Craigie

THE FOLCROFT PRESS, INC.

First Published 1940

Reprinted 1969

S. P. E.
TRACT No. LVI

THE GROWTH OF
AMERICAN ENGLISH

William A. Craigie

At the Clarendon Press

M DCCCCXL

THE GROWTH OF AMERICAN ENGLISH

I

WITH the steadily advancing compilation of the 'Dictionary of American English on Historical Principles', of which 1,140 pages have already been published by the University of Chicago Press, it is becoming possible to ascertain more precisely the proportion of new material with which the language has been enriched during the three centuries of existence and expansion in its new home, and to gain a clearer idea of the stages by which the new developments have successively taken place. While the main features by which the English of the United States has come to differ from that of Britain have been fully recognized in recent years, and have been increasingly illustrated in special works such as those of Schele de Vere, Mencken, Krapp, and Horwill, it is only in the light of the dated evidence now presented in the Dictionary that the full extent of the additions can be ascertained and seen in historical perspective. To illustrate this in some detail is the object of the present essay.

At the outset, however, it is necessary to state that the Dictionary, in spite of the wealth of material it contains, does not cover the whole of the American vocabulary. Of set purpose it does not attempt to include the whole body of American slang (and expressly excludes almost all of this that is of recent origin), and omits most of the words that are current only in local dialects and have made no appearance in literature. Neither of these fields could be satisfactorily dealt with except in special works, and a full historical dictionary of American slang would demand extensive collecting as well as an intimate first-hand knowledge of the subject.

The material included in the Dictionary may thus be regarded as mainly representative of the more serious and solid elements of American English, and in that respect as presenting a fair and adequate record of its special features and of the extent to which these are innovations and additions to the common tongue. This could not be done by confining attention to what could definitely be classed as Americanisms, since this would exclude a large number of words intimately associated with the development of the country and its institutions and with the history of the American people. Many English words, without acquiring a new meaning, have by force of circumstances become more significant for American life than they have ever been for British, and to ignore these would be to omit something truly characteristic and even national.

Bearing in mind then that the vocabulary included in the Dictionary represents American usage or currency on a much wider basis than that of American origin, it becomes a matter of interest to ascertain how many words, together with distinct senses of these or phrases containing them, naturally find a place in the work, what proportion among these the new bears to the old, and what the precise novelty is in each case. It may lie in the introduction of an entirely new word, either adopted from another language or apparently of spontaneous origin, or it may consist in adding a new sense to a word already in use, or sometimes in converting one part of speech into another, as making a noun into a verb or vice-versa.[1]

The former class—the absolutely new words—are easily distinguished, and few of any importance have escaped notice in the dictionaries or special works; the latter are often much less evident, and the American claim to them can only be substantiated by clear evidence of priority, such as the Dictionary frequently supplies. In this respect, however, a difficulty frequently arises in the shape of a doubt whether the evidence for this side of the Atlantic may not be defective. In many cases it undoubtedly is so, since the collecting on the American side was carried out on more intensive lines in a more limited field. Hence it is necessary to be cautious in assuming American priority on the basis of the available evidence, when there is no obvious reason for expecting the use to arise in the new country rather than the old. Such attributions have frequently been made without foundation,

---

[1] Various classifications of the different sources of American English have been made in the works dealing with the subject, e.g. Schele de Vere *Americanisms*, J. S. Farmer *Americanisms*, pp. ix–x, Clapin *New Dictionary of Americanisms*, pp. 424–505; Thornton *An American Glossary*, p. i; G. P. Krapp *History of the English Language in America*, H. L. Mencken *The American Language*. It is unnecessary here to enter into any enumeration of the details covered by these writers.

as Pickering now and then pointed out in his 'Vocabulary' of 1816, merely because the British or American writer did not happen to know the use as English. Thus in 1836 L. Matthews (*Lectures*, 127) wrote: 'Several words of American origin have within a few years struggled into good use in England; and, in spite of carping critics, have found their way to the bar, the senate, and the pulpit. Such are *organize*, *disorganize*, *demoralize*, and their verbal nouns *organization*, etc.' This is so far erroneous that both *organize* and *organization* are old in English, and were in common use from the later years of the eighteenth century, while *disorganize* was used by Burke in 1793. On the other hand, Webster's claim to have introduced *demoralize* into the language must be taken as valid until a British writer can be found anticipating his use of it in 1794: 'All wars have, if I may use a new but emphatic word, a demoralizing tendency.' The immediate source of this was no doubt the French *démoraliser* ('a word of the French revolution, admitted by the Academy 1798'), which apparently was not adopted by English writers before 1808.

Trusting entirely to such evidence as is readily available may in many cases lead to quite erroneous conclusions. A writer in the 'Boston Transcript' of 11 December 1897 claimed *dressmaker* for the United States, declaring that 'The evidence so far produced shows the word to be of American origin, like schooner, immigrant, and real-estate agent'. This statement had apparent justification in the article on the word in the O.E.D. (published in the previous July), which cited as the earliest authorities Webster's dictionary of 1828, and Washington Irving's 'Alhambra' of 1832, and in the fact that a dressmaker appeared in the Boston directory for 1821. Over against this, the earliest English evidence given was from 'Nicholas Nickleby' of 1838. Obviously the inference drawn from these dates was valid only if the evidence on both sides was complete, and no great research was necessary to find dressmakers in London in 1803 and in Liverpool in 1810, the latter being also the date of earliest American example in the new dictionary.

In some instances the relative datings run so close that no positive conclusion as to priority is possible. There is an American touch about *electioneer* and *electioneering* which is supported by a year's priority in date for the latter, but both words, as well as *electioneerer*, evidently came into use so contemporaneously in both countries that it would be hazardous to assume a British borrowing.

It is in connexion with attributive, adjectival, and other fixed collocations (as *cattle show, carriage-builder, civil service*), and phrases of various kinds, that the question of comparative dating most frequently arises, through the imperfections of the present English record. *Criminal court* has been in common American use from 1840, but no light on its English currency can be obtained from the dictionaries. 'Criminal Courts' is the heading of one of Dickens's 'Sketches by Boz' of 1835–6, but the phrase is not used in the text. To Scottish lawyers the distinction between civil and criminal courts had been familiar from the sixteenth century, but was unknown to their English colleagues. It was clearly introduced into English use by the Act of 25 July 1834 (Act 4–5 Will. IV, c. 36, § 1), the first section of which provided that the Lord Mayor, the Lord Chancellor, and others 'shall be the Judges of a Court to be called the "Central Criminal Court"'.

An interesting example of uncertain priority is that of *commercial traveller*. The earliest instance in the present record is from 1830 in the 'Journal of a Residence in London' by an American, N. S. Wheaton. Was he using a term already familiar to him, or one which he had learned in England, where it was about to replace the older 'bagman'? The latter alternative seems the more probable, since the distinctive name in America was 'drummer' (also recorded from 1830), and in 1841 there appeared at Glasgow a publication entitled 'The Commercial Travellers, by a Knight of the Whip'; the O.E.D. also provides a title from 1855 'The Commercial Traveller in Light and Shade'. In contrast to this the American evidence, according to the new dictionary, begins in 1870, but this again may be unduly late.

From 1701 to the present day the evidence for *dry goods* is so persistently American, and there are so many attributive uses, as *dry goods box, clerk, store*, &c., which are exclusively American, that any doubt regarding its origin might well seem superfluous. The Century Dictionary, however, cites it from a report of the House of Commons on smuggling, of the year 1745, which furnishes proof of English currency at that date, and makes it probable that it was known still earlier. It certainly was in Scotland, where it occurs in 1545 in the Burgh Records of Aberdeen (i. 213), along with the usual Scottish equivalent *dry ware*. The term is therefore clearly one of those which have become American by usage, although not so by origin.

The sections of the Dictionary now published, carrying it as far as *Gold region*, present so many examples of the various features of the American vocabulary, that even to summarize them would be an extensive task. It so happens, however, that the first two letters of the alphabet, A and B, are between them typical of all the rest in the kind of words they include, A containing many derived from Latin, while B abounds more in monosyllables of native origin. An analysis of these two letters, with due regard to considerations of space and interest, will therefore serve to bring out with sufficient clearness the nature of the information to be derived from the Dictionary as a whole.

In the 377 pages of A and B there are in all some 4,800 entries of separate words, and well over 7,000 of the various senses of these. Of this number about half (3,500) are marked with the sign +, which indicates that to all appearance they are of American origin, and thus form additions to the English vocabulary. These additions include many varieties which for the purpose of the present study need receive only general mention, since by their nature they do not admit of direct comparison with any corresponding term in English use. Such are the words—a limited number—adopted from other languages, especially Spanish (which has contributed some thirty in all) or topographical terms and adjectives derived from these, as *Alabama, Alabamian, Baltimore, Baltimorean, Boston, Bostonian*, &c. These form a numerous class, and enter into many special collocations as *Arkansas toothpick, Boston crackers, Bourbon whisky*. Another very extensive class consists of the composite names of plants and trees, animals, birds, and fishes, of the type *black alder, black bear, black bass*, &c. This adjective alone enters into about seventy such names, while *blue* accounts for sixty. The extent to which such names are entirely new formations is illustrated by those having *American* as the distinguishing adjective. Out of more than seventy of these only one, the *American aloe*, is earlier in English use, being mentioned by that name in Miller's dictionary of 1731.

Excluding these classes, important as they are in adding

so much new and distinctive material to the vocabulary, and confining attention to those words which more directly illustrate the relationship between the English of America and of Britain, it becomes clear that most of these fall under a few heads, of which all but one exemplify the creative tendency of American speech. This manifests itself in (1) the addition of new senses to existing words and phrases, (2) the formation of new derivative forms and attributive collocations or other compounds, (3) the introduction of words not previously in use (and not adopted from other languages of the American continent). A conservative tendency, keeping alive older uses, is illustrated by a much smaller number of words than is found in any of the other groups. The present section of this study treats only of the first of these classes; the others will form the subject of a later instalment.

A simple alphabetic array of the words coming under each of the various heads, with an indication of the date and nature of the new departure, would be both tedious and unenlightening. In the following survey a less mechanical arrangement is followed, based partly on the type of word and partly on the date at which the new usage appears; the miscellaneous nature of the material, however, makes it impossible to adhere strictly to any logical sequence. It is also necessary to state that the figures given for the different classes of words are well below the actual number which might be reckoned, as many examples of minor importance or limited currency have not been included.

I

There are at least 150 common words which have acquired new senses, and many of these have added more than one new meaning, some as many as five or six. They include all classes of words from the concrete to the abstract, and from the colloquial to the literary, the latter being especially noticeable in A. The majority are nouns, but verbs and adverbs are also well represented. It will be noticed that a fair number of the new senses appear as early as the seventeenth century, and that there are considerable additions before the end of the eighteenth, while the colloquial element becomes prominent in the nineteenth.

Among the earliest developments in nouns denoting material things, it is natural to find words designating natural features. One of the first of these to appear is *branch*, originally applied to one of the streams uniting to form a river, but soon (from 1663) used as a name for a small stream or brook by itself. 'He proceeded cautiously towards a rivulet, or in the vernacular of the country, a *branch*, that meandered along the foot of the hill', says a writer of 1833. A similar early change in the meaning of *creek* has been frequently noticed.

The case of *bluff* is of special interest. Originally a nautical adjective, applied to the bows of a ship when nearly vertical, it had by 1658 been extended to describe a steep bank or shore. In 1687 it appears in South Carolina as a noun in the latter sense, is rare before 1700, but common after that date. For some time it was confined to South Carolina and Georgia, and many of the early instances refer to the town of Savannah, where John Wesley found it in established use in 1737. 'Savannah stands on a flat bluff, so they term any high land hanging over a creek or river.' By 1776 its use had spread to New England, and before 1800 to the Mississippi, later becoming general throughout the West.

Boundary, in addition to its usual meaning, came as early as 1670 to be used in the sense of a 'bound mark' (1640) or 'bound tree' (1663), as in 'a tree marked N.F., being a boundary between Wethersfield and Hertford', and 'a great stone laid close by a rock is the boundary of my upper division'.

Other examples of similar developments are: *Barren*, as a noun, usually in the plural *barrens*, used from 1697 as a name for tracts of land having little or no vegetation except small trees or shrubs.   *Bog*, from 1714 as a small hummock or tussock in a bog, marsh, or wet meadow, a sense which may well puzzle the English reader in such sentences as 'he strode and jumped from one bog to another'. Hence the verb *to bog* may mean to remove hummocks in a meadow. *Bench*, from 1811, for an elevated level stretch of ground, a natural terrace, between a river-bank and higher ground, or on a mountain side, whence also the later compound *benchland*. *Bald* (1838–), a bare or treeless mountain top, especially in the Southern Appalachians, where it sometimes occurs as a proper name. This is a natural extension of the use in *bald hill*, &c., which in English is as old as 1642.   *Bay* (1850–), a part of a prairie extending into, and almost

surrounded by, wood or forest. This is quite distinct from
an earlier Southern *bay*, a piece of low marshy ground pro-
ducing large numbers of bay-trees. South Carolina 'abounds
in bays, swamps, and drains', Anbury wrote in 1795. Of a
less usual type is *alkali* (1870–), extended from the chemical
ingredient of the soil in south-western areas to the land or
region characterized by it, common in such sentences as
'the ponies had done the alkali for three days', and even
applied to one living in such a region; 'a white-faced woman
who looked mighty good to us alkalis opened the door'.

Examples based on verbs are: *Boil* (1805–), one of those
places in the Mississippi where 'the water rises with a strong
circular motion', also described as 'immense upheavings of
the moving waters'. *Burn* (1846–), a place where the trees,
brush, or grass have been burned, a clearing in the woods
or on the prairie resulting from this; the deer 'resort always
to a recent burn, when grass and weeds are just shooting
again'. *Blow-out* (1892–), in the West, a hollow made by
the wind in an area of loose sand, or on the top of a
'butte'.

Alley, in addition to its ordinary sense (for which however
the purely American *alleyway* is commonly used), has
become specialized as the distinctive name of a narrow lane
lying between, and running parallel to, two streets, and giving
access to the rear of the houses or other buildings on each
side of it. This use, which can be traced back in the records
of Baltimore to 1729, is exemplified in 'each block of lots
has the advantage of two sixteen feet alleys'. A later application (1833–) is that to an open passage left in a field or crop
to facilitate cultivation. Contrasted with the alley is the
avenue (1780–), a wide or principal street, a broad through-
fare, common in the larger American cities.

A connected or compact group of houses or other buildings
was called a *block* from 1796 onwards; in Washington (1801)
'the buildings are brick, and erected in what are called large
blocks, that is, from two to five or six houses, joined together,
and appear like one long building'. Similarly a number of
'lots' bounded by streets was 'a block of lots' (1815–17) or
simply 'a block' (1823–), which has become the usual term
for one of the rectangular areas in which towns are usually
laid out; 'the village had been formally laid out into the
streets and blocks that resembled a city'. The regularity of

these has naturally led to the word being used as a measure of distance in a town (1843–), as in 'he walked five blocks in a rain-storm'.

Still another application of *block* (1829–52) was as a shortening of *blockhouse*, the latter again being used not only in its older sense (common from the early seventeenth century to the latter part of the nineteenth), but also in that of a house built of squared logs (1821–57) differing from a *log-house*, in which the logs were 'hewn only within, having the bark on the outside'. By a similar dropping of 'house', *brick* by itself came to denote a brick building (1845–), as in 'a three-story brick', 'the great excess of new bricks over new frame buildings'. In a frame-building an important part of the structure was the *bent* (1815–), 'a section of the frame which is put together on the ground or foundation and then raised by holding the feet of the posts and elevating the upper portion'. An exciting account of the raising of 'a bent' is given by Fenimore Cooper in his novel 'The Chainbearer'.

Further examples of words belonging to this group are: *Armory* (1794–), a factory for the making of arms. *Barn* (1828–), a stable as well as a storehouse, e.g. 'thieves entered the barn and stole a chestnut mare'. *Aisle* (1827–), a passage-way in a building, store, &c., or (1842–) in a railway carriage or street car. *Altar* (1820–), an enclosed space at the front in a church or at an open-air meeting.

Among words connected with rivers and transport or travel on these may be noted: *Bent* (1669–1770), a bend or curve in a river. *Boom*, a barrier placed to retain floating logs while these are being collected, possibly as old as the seventeenth century, but quite clearly in use from 1789, when the Massachusetts Acts mention 'the laying of a boom across the river . . . for the purpose of stopping and securing logs and other lumber'. *Ark* (1759–), a large rectangular, flat-bottomed boat used on the larger rivers, such as the Ohio and Mississippi, especially in the latter part of the eighteenth century and the early years of the nineteenth; 'in the year 1825 more than eight hundred and forty large arks . . . passed down the Susquehanna River'. *Battery* (1841–), a boat used in shooting wild ducks, or a special screen fitted up on one. *Birch* (1861–) as an abbreviation for birch-bark canoe. 'Never use the word *canoe* if you wish to retain your respect. *Birch* is the term among us back-woodsmen' (Lowell).

The noun *blaze*, which in English denoted a white mark on the face of a horse, was retained in that sense, but was also applied to a similar mark made on a tree by slicing off part of the bark, and serving either as a boundary mark or to point out a path in the forest. In this sense it has been in common use from 1662 to the present day, especially in the latter connexion. 'The trail is a series of plain blazes on the trees which any one could follow.'   *Blade*, used naturally of the leaf of maize, had become specialized in that sense by 1800; 'during the winter they kept their horses on blades'.   *Bush* (also used, though less frequently, in the same sense as in the British colonies) was specially applied (1823–54) to a grove of sugar-maple trees, or the place in the forest where the making of maple-sugar was carried on.

The use of *buffalo* as a name for the North American bison came as early as 1635, and was common even before acquain-tance had been made with the vast herds of the western prairies. By natural ellipse it also came to denote buffalo meat (1743–), the buffalo fish (1788–), and a buffalo robe (1835–), the latter puzzling the British traveller who was asked if he wanted a couple of buffaloes for his excursion and replied that he would rather have horses.   *Buck*, in addi-tion to remaining in use for a male deer, is also used in place of 'ram' (1812–), perhaps under the influence of German *bock* and *schafbock*. Other new applications are those to a male Indian (1850–) or negro (1880–), and (1845–) by ellipse for *buckshot* (which is itself of American origin); 'the doctor drew a bird charge from his gun and loaded it with buck'. The compound *buckskin* was by transference applied to one wearing garments of this material, originally and usually a Virginian (1745–), and to a horse of the colour of buckskin (1889–); 'the splendid buckskins, the best horses in camp'.

Among words denoting persons singly or collectively are: *Brave*, an Indian warrior (1819–), familiar to all readers of novels or other works relating to the red man, and at a later date (1871–) a member of the Tammany Society, whose 'organization was supposed in a general way to imitate Indian customs'.   *Boy*, a male negro slave (1764–); 'they always address as "boy" and "girl" ... all under forty years of age'. *The boys* are successively loungers about taverns, town loafers (1834–), men in the army during the Civil War (1861–), frequent in 'the boys in blue', and political followers or hangers on (1885–). *Brigade* (1836–), a band of trappers or hunters; 'the hunter never goes alone. He and his friends and neighbours make up a brigade—large or small, it is called a brigade.' *Butcher*, which has acquired the curious senses of a copy-reader in a newspaper office (1867–), and the man or boy who sells sweets, fruit, &c., on a railway train (*a* 1889–). *Bloat* (*a* 1861–), a bloated person, a drunkard; 'the veriest bloat and bully in the company'.

Among national or racial designations *Anglo-Indian* (1812–45), applied to American Indians allied with the English, may have anticipated the ordinary British use. The extended use of *Anglo-Saxon*, to include whatever is distinctive of the English people or culture at home or abroad, appears to be originally American (as adjective from 1832, as noun from 1846), and due to a natural desire to avoid the limitation which might be implied in 'English'. It is obvious that the latter term could not be used in such a sentence as 'The Anglo-Saxon never can acknowledge the corn to the cross of negro and Indian'. The extension of *African* to any American negro, whether brought from Africa or born in the country, is natural enough, but in certain contexts may completely puzzle the English reader, as when a member of Congress, speaking on the Army Appropriation Bill of 1879, is reported as saying, 'There is a gigantic African here. . . . I want the African taken out of the bill.' To his hearers this was plain enough, *African* being a mere equivalent of *nigger* in the phrase 'a nigger in the woodpile', used to imply something concealed or underhand.

As miscellaneous examples of words denoting things a considerable number call for notice. The following paragraphs are based on a rough grouping of these according to the character of the object.

Belt (1661–), as applied to the Indian belt of wampum, used especially as a token of friendship, and hence called 'a belt of peace'. *Blanket* (1704–) in its use as a garment by Indians not yet assimilated in dress to the white man; hence 'to say of one's father or mother that they wore the blanket implies that they were but half-civilized Indians', and 'blanket Indians' (1859–) as a designation for these. *Bishop* as a lady's bustle, from 1787 to 1848, and *Arctic* (1878–)

a waterproof shoe, frequently fur-lined, worn as a protection against cold and wet.

Bit (1688–), a small Spanish silver coin or an equivalent of this, and latterly, especially in the West, a nominal coin or amount of the value of twelve and a half cents, two bits being equal to a quarter dollar. This was originally a translation of the Spanish *pieza*, but its currency was no doubt furthered by the habit of cutting silver coins into pieces to obtain smaller units.   *Bulk* (1678–), a pile of tobacco made up to undergo sweating.   *Box* (1720–), a cavity made in the trunk of a tree for collecting maple-sap or turpentine. *Boll* (1796–) as the seed-vessel of the cotton-plant, which in English use had been applied to that of flax or the poppy.

Biscuit (1818–), applied to a variety of small soft scone, the original biscuit having become a *cracker*, although some manufacturing firms still call them biscuits.   *Burgoo*, originally a sailor's name for a thick oatmeal gruel or porridge, but in the southern States from 1853 applied to a highly-seasoned soup of meat and vegetables, 'popular in Kentucky and other places, especially at barbecues, picnics, and other outdoor feasts'.   *Butter* (1864–), but earlier in *apple-butter*, 1819–), a preparation of fruit or other suitable substance cooked to a butter-like consistency and used for similar purposes.

Bureau (1751–), transferred from a writing-desk with drawers to an ordinary chest of drawers, usually surmounted by an adjustable mirror; 'it occurred to him that the garment had gotten into the drawer of a bureau that stood in the corner'.   *Box* (1838–), a pigeon-hole or receptacle in a post-office in which the subscriber's postal matter is placed; also (1859–), a kind of boat used in duck-shooting; the body of a wagon (1886–), and the station occupied by the pitcher in baseball (1886–).   *Block* (1853–), the stand on which slaves stood when being sold by auction; 'the negroes were to be put on the block next morning'.

Bow, in the plural *bows* (1711–), the rims of a pair of spectacles, as in Longfellow's 'Glasses with horn bows sat astride of his nose'; and, much later (1863–), the bent strips of wood supporting the canvas tilt of a 'covered wagon'. *Bead* (1831–), the small round knob on a thin stem forming the front sight of a gun, whence the common phrase, 'to draw a bead on' in the sense of 'to take aim at'.   *Button*

(1838–), the hard bone-like structure at the end of the rattles of a rattlesnake; also (1869–), a rounded mass of metal. *Battery* (1833–), the smallest pan of the set used in sugar-boiling, and (1853–) a set of stamps for pounding ore in a stamp-mill.   *Blossom* (1819–), radiated quartz, in full 'blossom of quartz or mineral blossom'; also (1881–) the oxidized or decomposed outcrop of a vein or coal-bed, occurring earlier in *blossom-rock* (1872–).   *Brick* (1869–), a rectangular block of silver or gold, common in the figurative *gold-brick*; 'they would swap the talent for a gold brick and lose the napkin'.

Armour, steel plating for war vessels, apparently of American origin, and clearly known by that name from 1838, but according to Knight suggested in 1812.   *Bumper* (1839–), a buffer for railway carriages, and (1860–) a cradle or rocker used in gold-mining.   *Bob* (1844–), an attachment to the tail of a kite, serving to balance it in the air.

Bunch has developed quite a number of special senses, as a clump of trees (1683–1742), the hump of a buffalo (1733–48), a swarm of bees (1782), a pile of boards or a bundle of shingles (1845–), and a herd of cattle, horses, or other animals (1864–); 'I nearly always find them at home, looking after their little bunches of stock'.

To words of a more abstract type belong: *Bill* (1682–), a government note or a bank-note, first proposed and introduced in Massachusetts; also, in recent use (1881–), an order to a saw-mill for wood cut to specified sizes, whence *bill-stuff* for wood so ordered.   *Bounty* (1728–), a reward given in return for the killing of wild animals or Indians. A little earlier, in 1718, the payment of a bounty to the 'Northern colonies' to encourage their export of 'naval stores' to Britain was suggested by the English writer William Wood, and this being carried into effect immediately afterwards was apparently the origin of such commercial bounties.   *Betterment* (1785–), an improvement made on real property, first used in Vermont, 'but it has for a long time' says Pickering in 1816, 'been common in the State of New Hampshire, and it has been getting into use in some parts of Massachusetts, since the passing of the late law, similar to the Betterment Acts (as they are called) of the states above mentioned'. *Balance* (1788–), the remainder or rest of anything, a use frequently commented on, by both British and American writers, in the first half of the nineteenth century, and even later. 'I doubt', Professor Freeman wrote in 1883, 'whether any one in England would talk of the "balance of the day", a phrase which I have heard in America'. Among the early examples given in the Dictionary are 'the balance of our things', 'the balance of nine deer that had been killed', 'I spent a part of the evening at a friend's house, and the balance at home', 'we walked through the balance of the hospital', all by 1826. *Backbone* (1857–), strength or firmness of character, 'moral stamina, strength of will, firmness of purpose. A figurative expression recently much used in political writings' (Bartlett 1859). *Bottom* (1867–), the foundation or basis on which a state of things, a financial project or other scheme rests, common in the phrase 'the bottom has dropped out of (something)' or equivalents of this; also (1869–), the lowest point, figure, or price, as in 'logs touched bottom,' or the lowest point, during the summer of 1868'. *Bureau* (1831–, after French usage), a sub-division of a branch of the Federal government, as in the Indian Bureau, Pension Bureau, Meteorological Bureau.

The two verbal nouns *beat* and *break* have, like *bunch*, developed a striking variety of new uses.

Beat, appearing earlier (1721–) than in the English record (1825–) in the sense of a regular round or route, as of a person on duty, has from this in Alabama and Mississippi acquired that of a division of a county, a voting precinct (1860–). It is also used of a path or track made by animals (1838–; possibly 1736). *The beat of* (1833–) means anything to surpass or excel the thing in question, especially, in such expressions as 'I never saw (or heard) the beat of that'. In journalism (1875–) *a beat* is the feat of securing and publishing a piece of news before one's rivals, or the item of news itself. Applied to persons a *beat* denotes one who is lazy, shiftless, or broken down (1870–, more emphatically a *dead-beat*, 1863–), or one who departs without paying his bills (1887–).

Break is equally prolific in new applications, viz. in the West, a sharp interruption in the terrain, chiefly in the plural *breaks* (1854–); a disturbed area on the surface of water, such as that made by the rising of a fish or by a snag (1852–); a regular sale of tobacco at the 'breaking' or opening of the hogsheads (1859–); a rush or dash away from a place (1833–)

or *for* a place or person (1845–), also an attempt or try *at* something (1886); a breakdown or failure (1827–); a sudden fall in the price of stocks on the stock exchange (1870–); a sudden change in the gait or speed of a horse, especially a racehorse (1868–); a mistake or error, usually 'a bad break' (1884–); a critical or decisive point or moment (1888–).

The nouns so far considered are mainly of a colloquial or familiar type, and the majority are monosyllables, such as occur freely in the spoken tongue and readily lend themselves to new uses. The new developments in American English are far from being confined to words of this class, but include many of a more learned or literary character, belonging especially to the Latin element of the language. These are naturally more prominent in A than in B, as will be evident from the following examples, which for convenience include a few verbs as well as nouns. There being little connexion between any of these, they are here arranged according to the date at which they show, or begin to show, the addition of new senses.

Accommodation (1636–84), a grant of land made to a colonist, as in 'the best situation for farms and accommodations', 'his whole accommodation, both upland and meadow'. Also (1824–) financial aid in an emergency, a loan (along with the verb *accommodate* from 1811, to furnish a person with a loan, 'a commercial sense' according to Webster). By ellipse, equivalent to an 'accommodation' stage coach (1829–) or train (1877–); 'they boarded the single passenger car of the accommodation'. *Addition* (1636–1721), a lot or piece of land added to a previous holding, as in 'to lay out the addition of land granted to Mr. A.'; also (1638–), a new part added to a building, and (1786–) an area recently laid out as an extension of the residential section of a town. This latter sense is first recorded in such contexts as 'Howard's new addition to Baltimore Town', but a century later is called 'a trans-Mississippi word'.

Agency (1707–), specialized as the office or position of an Indian agent (see p. 216); also (1796–), the area under the charge or control of an Indian agent, and (1824–) the headquarters of the agent, a station or fort serving as such in an Indian territory or reservation. *Appropriation* (1761–), the action of setting apart a sum of money for a special purpose, or the sum so assigned, now long current as the

2275.56

Q

normal sense of the word, not cited in English use before 1858. *Admission* (together with the verb *admit*), used for the granting to a barrister or attorney of authority to practice (1766–), and for the formal acceptance of a State as part of the Union (1777–), which is celebrated in some of the western States by a legal holiday known as 'admission day'. *Appreciation* (1777–), an increase in value or amount, 'rather an appreciation of gold and silver than a depreciation of paper', and in line with this the verb *appreciate*, used both transitively and intransitively, to raise or rise in value. The intransitive use, admitted by Webster, was rejected by a purist of 1809; 'this is not, we believe, found in a single English author, and in the United States is only admitted into genteel company by inadvertence'. *Assumption* (1789–), the adoption or taking over of obligations, and especially the taking over of the State debts by the Federal government after the War of Independence. *Apportionment* (1791–), the assignment, on the basis of population, of the number of representatives that each State may send to the House of Representatives, or that each district may send to the State legislature; also (1778–), the assignment of direct taxes on the basis of population.

Address (1822–), a formal request, directed to the executive by both branches of the legislature, requesting the removal of a judge; hence (from the same date) *to address out*, to get a judge removed in this way. *Amalgamation* (1839–), with the verb *amalgamate* (1859–), 'universally applied, in the United States, to the mixing of the black and white races' (Bartlett). *Appointment* (1847–), 'a part in the exercises of an exhibition or commencement' given as an honour to a student who has attained distinction in his work, and who thus becomes an *appointee*. *Affiliation*, with the verb *affiliate* (1852–), denoting association or alliance in politics or some other activity; 'Can we affiliate with the Whigs? Never!' 'A citizen of opposite political affiliations.' The verb also (1877–) has the sense of 'to combine', as one substance or element with another.

To this group may be added two verbs and two adjectives. *Average* (1769–), to be on an average, defined by Webster as 'to form a mean or medium sum or quantity', a use not recorded in English before 1814. The earliest American example cited is from the diary of George Washington, 'a fat wether . . . that would average the above weight'.   *Avail* (*a* 1781–1840), used transitively, to give or afford one the knowledge, benefit, or advantage of something; 'it will rest with you to avail Mr. B. of that fund',—one of the Americanisms pointed out by Dr. Witherspoon.   *Available* (1837–), of a political candidate, having the requisite influence or other qualification likely to ensure election; even in American use frequently distinguished by quotation marks. Hence *availability* (1844–), defined by Bartlett (1848) as 'that qualification in a candidate which implies or supposes a strong probability of his success, apart from substantial merit—a probability resulting from mere personal or accidental popularity'.   *Academical* (1813–) and *Academic* (1856–), applied to that department of a college or university which deals with classical, mathematical, and general literary studies as distinguished from the technical or professional.

A few nouns of this class represent more concrete objects or concepts.   *Advance*, in military use (1780–), an advance guard (in American use from 1758 in place of the earlier English 'advanced guard').   *Annuity* (1797–), a yearly payment in money or provisions made by the United States to a group or tribe of Indians; in 1849, says a writer, 'the Indian thinks only of annuities and goods, instead of war and plunder'.   *Athenæum* (1807–), 'an association of persons of literary or scientific tastes, for the purpose of mutual improvement' (Webster); also (1818–), a room or building in which books, magazines, and newspapers are kept for the use of members or the public.   *Artery* (1827–), the chief river of a river-system, as 'the mighty arteries of the Missouri and the Mississippi'; also (1850–) a main line in any branching system of communication, as 'those great arteries of commerce—the railroads'.   *Ardent*, by ellipse (1835–), also in the plural *ardents*, ardent spirits; 'water mixed with a little of the ardent'.   *Artificial* (1842–), an artificial flower; 'a yellow bonnet with a great pink artificial on it'. *Ambulance* (1860–), in the West, a type of travelling or touring vehicle, resembling a hospital ambulance; 'a private party in prairie ambulances'.   *Apartment* (1876–), a set of rooms among other sets in a building, originally synonymous with 'flat', but latterly either displacing this or regarded as implying something superior.   *Avoirdupois* (1861–), personal weight, as in 'we lightened the canoe by two men's avoirdupois', 'a woman of solid avoirdupois'. This is certainly independent of Shakespeare's solitary instance of *haber-de-pois* in the same sense.

Bailiwick (*a* 1647–) came, at least as early as 1700, to be a district in which the authority was vested in a sheriff in place of a bailie. In this sense it remained current into the nineteenth century, and has given rise to the common phrase 'out of one's bailiwick', i.e. outside of one's natural sphere or function. *Barony*, adopted by Locke in his Constitution for Carolina in 1669 as a division of a county, had a shorter career, apparently surviving only into the first half of the eighteenth century.

There are a few examples of new or special meanings being attached to personal designations. *Assistant* (1629–), though originating in England, became the distinctive name of an executive and judicial officer in New England during the first century of the colonies there. *Agent* (1646–) was down to the Revolution the title of the person appointed by the various colonies to represent their interests in London; from 1707 it also became equivalent to 'Indian agent', one who acted as the representative of the government in matters concerning it and an Indian tribe. Later on it includes a station-agent or ticket-agent (1835–) and a 'road-agent' or highwayman (1881–), while New York in 1877 appointed an 'agent of truancy' to enforce attendance at school. *Article* (1837–) became a personal designation by being commonly applied to a slave, who might be attractively described as 'a first-rate article'.

Burgess was at a very early date (1619) adopted as the designation of a member of the legislative bodies in Maryland and Virginia, and remained in use till the Revolution. Later (1821–) it took on the meaning of councillor or magistrate in a borough or township. The use of *baron* to designate a magnate in commerce or finance appears in 1885 in 'silver barons', to which 'lumber barons', 'cattle barons', and many more are naturally added.

Unusual applications are found in: *Brahmin* (1861–) used, originally by Oliver Wendell Holmes, with 'caste' as a satirical name for the upper class of New Englanders, and sub-sequently (1881–) by itself to denote a member of this. *Bourbon* (1871–), a conservative in politics, especially a democrat of old-fashioned or conservative principles, in allusion to the royal family of France, regarded as learning nothing by experience. *Argonaut* (1873–), one of those adventurers who went to California immediately after the discovery of gold there in 1848, otherwise known as 'forty-miners'.

The ordinary colloquial verbs to which new senses have been given come almost entirely under the letter B. The earliest appears to be *bind* (1677–), which by a grammatical confusion took on the meaning of *bound*, to lie in boundary with, to border on, a place, found in general use as late as 1832, 'lots binding on the Ohio River', and surviving locally to 1899 or later. Others are: *Box* (1700–), to make an incision in the trunk of a tree in order to collect the sap or turpentine; 'the trees are boxed and tapped early in the year'. *Bank* (1720–), to protect a cellar, house, barn, &c., especially against the cold of winter, by piling earth against it; also (1856–), to stack or pile up logs on a river-bank to await removal. *Brush* (1755–), to force on, to drive hard or briskly; the intransitive use, to ride, run, or move quickly, appears earlier in English use (1805) than in the U.S. (1833). *Beat*, in the past participle with *out* (1758–), worn out by fatigue, exhausted; 'she's clear beat out; she must go to bed this minute'; later, in the infinitive, &c., to get the better of by trickery, to cheat or defraud, and in the phrase *to beat one's way* (1887–), to travel by train without paying one's fare. *Bundle* (1781–), of the two sexes, to occupy the same bed without undressing, implied a little earlier in *bundler* (1774–); the practice of *bundling*, naturally much commented on by those to whom it was novel, was reported as still in use in 1888 'in a few isolated localities'. *Bed* (1792–), to furnish a tree with a bed to fall on when felled, 'a contrivance which they call *bedding* the tree'; also (1830–), to plough ground in beds, especially for cotton, and with *down* (1888–) to collect cattle on the plains and guard them till they lie down to sleep, or of the cattle (1903–), to lie down for the night. These uses are interesting as representing successively the industries of lumbering, farming, and cattle-raising. *Break* (1809), of a hunting dog, to chase game too far ahead, also (1834–) of dogs, cattle, or persons, to make a rush or dash, frequently with *for* a place or thing, as 'we broke for our arms, they for theirs'. Further (1852–) of a horse, especially in racing, to change gait, especially

from a level to an uneven stride; (1885–) of fish, to come to
the surface of the water; (1885–) to cause a sharp fall in
prices, or (1892–) of prices, &c., to fall sharply or suddenly.
In the sense of preparing land for cultivation by ploughing
or digging (1846–) the simple verb takes the place of the
earlier 'break up'.   *Brace*, with *up* (1809–), to take liquor
or a tonic to give vigour to the nerves or system, and (1816–)
to pull oneself together, to prepare for an effort; also (1846–)
to press or plant firmly, as 'with his feet firmly braced against
the dash-board'.   *Belt* (1812–), to 'girdle' a tree, to cut
through (and remove) the bark in order to kill it; 'the beaver,
in technical language, belts them with his teeth'.   *Belong*
(1821–), to have a natural connexion or association with
something, to be in its (or one's) proper place or sphere, as
'to replace it where it belongs', 'he belonged out of doors'.
Buckle, with *to* (1825–), to lay hold of, to apply oneself *to* a
thing; also with *down to* (1865–), to settle down to, to work
steadily or seriously at something, and with *in* (1828–) 'to
close in, to embrace or seize the body in a scuffle. A popular
use in America' (Webster).   *Begin*, with a preceding
negative and followed by an infinitive (1833–), to make
any, or the least, approach to be or do something, as 'we
can't begin to come up to the prospectus'; also, by
ellipse, to compare at all *with* something.   *Bark* (1831–),
to kill a squirrel by striking the bark of the tree immediately below it with a bullet.   *Bolt* (1833–), to break
away from a political party or its representative, to desert
or go over to the opposite party; also transitively (1847–),
to desert a party, candidate, or programme. Hence *bolt*
as a noun (1858–), *bolter* (1858–), and *bolting* (1845–),
all in common use.   *Burst* (1833–), to fail financially,
to go bankrupt, and transitively (1850–), to reduce to
insolvency, to break. These senses are equally common
in the colloquial form *bust* from 1840 and 1837 respectively.   *Brush* with *up* (1840–), to make oneself more
neat and tidy, and figuratively, to refresh one's memory
or revise one's knowledge of a subject; 'if you wish to brush
up on your English you will find nothing better'.   *Back*
(1840–), to carry on the back; 'the Indians back heavy loads,
confined by a strap over their foreheads'.   *Bulldog* (1842–),
to attack or assail like a bulldog; in Western usage, to seize
and throw an animal in a particular way.   *Boom* (1852–),

of a river, to rush strongly, said also of logs carried down by a river; hence (1873–), to display sudden activity or briskness, to rise rapidly in prosperity or importance, and transitively (1882–), to bring prominently into public notice, to support or advertise strongly. Hence also the nouns *boom* (1879), *boomer* (1882), and *booming* (1873). *Bill* (1867–), to enter goods on a way-bill, to consign by rail to a destination; also (1863–) to cover a town by distributing or fixing up bills or posters, 'we had billed the town pretty well'. *Board* (1875–), to keep and feed horses as well as persons, 'the mare was boarded out of town'; also (1879–), by transference from boarding a vessel, to get on or go into a train or car. *Bounce* (1877–), to eject forcibly, to throw out, and figuratively (1876–) to discharge or dismiss summarily from an employment or post, and (1893–) to reject a suitor. *Blanket* (1892–), to include under one head or category, to take inclusively; 'the employees then holding office were not blanketed into the service'.

From A only two instances need be cited. *Approach* (1833–), to steal up to an animal or herd in hunting, in order to get within range; also (1857–), to make overtures to a person with the object of influencing him. In both senses the noun *approach* also occurs, but more rarely. *Allow* (1825–), to declare, maintain, think or believe; 'he allowed he was doing his religious duties'. The late and slight appearance of this use in English dialects (1875) makes American origin probable.

Certain adverbs and prepositions have acquired either special senses or greater currency. *Below* (1645–), at or to a lower point on a river, lower down, as 'his course like theirs seemed to lie below'; also (1711–), off a port or shore. *Around* (1776–), freely used in various contexts where the normal English word would be *round* or *about*, e.g. 'it is told around for a fact', 'to hang around a person', 'there isn't any getting around that'. *Aside* in place of the English 'apart', in *aside from* (1818–), in addition to, without including, besides, as 'aside from the lumber it cost $15,000 to build it', and (1861–) except for, as 'aside from those cuts the marble is very sound. *Away* in such phrases as *away down* (1825–), *away up* (1834–), *away back* (1882–, referring to time); also denoting 'to a great extent, far', as in 'manufacturers are away behind in their deliveries'. *Ahead* with *of* (1825–), in advance of another or others in respect of progress, prosperity, success, &c., or without 'of' (1828–), in an advanced or leading position or successful state. *To go ahead* (1833–) was in early use distinguished by quotation marks, and by some attributed to David Crockett, which appears to be possible.   *Along* in the phrases *to get along* (1830–), to get on, to manage, especially in circumstances not too easy or favourable (a use noted as an Americanism by British travellers); *to be along* (1831–), to come to a place, to call; *along back* (1851–), for some time recently; *right along* (1856–), continuously, without interruption. Also in various applications to time, as 'far along in the day', 'along about eleven o'clock', 'I am well along', i.e. advanced in years; and by ellipse (1773–), in company with another or others, as 'our captain's wife was not along', 'there were half a dozen wagons along'.   *Aboard* in the conductor's call *all aboard* (1837–), latterly used to direct passengers to enter a train or street-car about to start, and by itself (1855–) as adverb and preposition = on or into a train, &c., also in the fuller form *on board* (1860–).

A few applications of common adjectives and adverbs are new.   *Blooded* (1778–), of horses or other animals, of good blood, of a pure or superior breed or stock, 'my blooded colts are of the finest breed in Virginia'; also (1804–) occasionally applied to persons.   *Back* (1779–), pertaining to past time, in arrears, overdue, as 'back allowance', 'back rent', 'making up back lessons', especially common with *taxes* (1788–), *pay* (1865–), and *salary* (1873–).   *Bright* with *look out* (1781–), a good or sharp look out. Also (1822–) applied to a quality of tobacco, and (1831–) to the complexion of light-coloured mulattoes. The adverbial *bright and early* appears in common use from 1837.   *Awful* (1809–), very unpleasant or disagreeable, extremely ugly or objectionable, a New England use brought into notice in the early years of the nineteenth century, commented on by Pickering and others, and recognized as an Americanism by Lamb in 1822, 'she is indeed, as the Americans would express it, something awful'. Also (1843–) as a mere intensive, 'woodmen sharp-set are awful eaters'; this however appears in English use at virtually the same date. The adverb *awfully* in the first of these senses is also mentioned by Pickering in 1816, and both this and *awful* (1818–) become common as mere intensives.

Bully (1844–), fine, capital, first rate; also (1869–) used adverbially, 'the old man is doing bully'.   *Balky* (1856–), of a horse or mule, given to stopping suddenly and refusing to go on.

In a few instances (as in *bright and early* above) the novelty is not in the words themselves but in the phrases formed from them. Among these are: *Basket of chips* (1800–), used in comparisons of which the most usual is 'smiling (or pleasant) as a basket of chips'.   *Book* in 'to talk like a book' (1829–) and 'to know like a book' (1839–), both apparently having American priority in date.   *Ball and chain* (1835–), the iron ball and the chain attaching it to a prisoner's leg to prevent escape, common in reference to working gangs of prisoners.   *Brick* in 'like a thousand of brick, or bricks' (1842–), and 'to have a brick in one's hat' (1847–), to be intoxicated.   *Blood and thunder*, used attrib. (1857–) with 'novel', 'story', &c., to designate low-class fiction or drama abounding in bloodshed and violence.   *Bone*, in 'to feel it in one's bones' (1857–, but earlier 'it was in my bones', 1844), to feel certain about, to have an intuitive knowledge of, something.   *Back*, in 'to get one's back up' (1854–), where 'get' is used in place of the English 'set' or 'put'.   *Blockade*, in 'to run the blockade' (1861–), giving rise almost immediately to *blockade-runner* (1863–) and *-running* (1864–).

New uses of verbs are in part created by the addition of adverbs. *Back down*, to descend backwards, used literally in 1849, but figuratively by 1859, when Bartlett defined it as 'to withdraw a charge, eat one's own words'.   *Blaze away* (1776–) and *bang away* (1840–) as synonyms of 'fire away' (English from 1775), both in common use, and the former also figurative from 1834.   *Board* with *out* (1774–), to obtain meals outside of one's home or lodgings, and with *round* either transitively (1833–), to furnish a schoolmaster with board in different houses in turn, or more frequently intransitive (1839–) of the schoolmaster, to obtain board in this manner.

Two nautical phrases have become popular in figurative senses. *Backing and filling* (literal in 1777) takes on the sense (1841–) of alternately receding and advancing in action or policy, vacillating or hesitating; 'that turned out well, notwithstanding the backing and filling of the lawyers and owners'.   *By and large* (1769–), common in the sense of 'on the whole, in a general way, generally speaking', originally and usually with *take* or *taking*; 'taking them by and large, the French people have a wider command of their mother-tongue . . . than have the American people in relation to the English language' was the opinion of an American writer in 1901.

This array of ordinary English words from only two letters of the alphabet, covering possibly one tenth of the total vocabulary, illustrates in a striking manner the extent to which the language in America, during the three centuries of its existence there, has been enriched from its own resources without requiring to add a new word or even a new compound. The equally extensive role played by the formation of new compounds and collocations remains to be exhibited in the second portion of this study.

THE GROWTH OF AMERICAN ENGLISH

II

THE first part of this study (Tract No. LVI) was devoted to illustrating by copious examples from the first two letters of the alphabet how much in the development of American English was due to 'the addition of new senses to existing words or phrases'. Equally fertile has been the further process of 'the formation of new derivative forms and attributive collocations or other compounds'. The following illustration of these is also limited to the same two letters, which afford ample material for the purpose. In the majority of instances it will be readily noted that the new derivative or collocation has arisen quite naturally from circumstances or conditions peculiar to American life or its surroundings, and that the resulting form or expression is one not normally required in the language of the British Isles, though perfectly in keeping with English usage and analogues. Sometimes, however, the innovation has been found so apt and useful that at a later date it has been adopted by British writers and speakers, and in time has been accepted in ordinary use, and in the end without any suspicion of its American origin.

I

To begin with examples of new derivatives or compounds. The abolition of slavery began to be a serious question almost simultaneously (1787–8) in England and America, and to all appearance the derivatives *abolitionist* (1790) and *abolitionism* (1808) are earlier in English than American use (1834). The question, however, ceased to have a practical interest in England after 1833, whereas it assumed increasing importance in the United States down to the Civil War. Hence it is natural that various other derivatives should have arisen there, viz. *abolitional* (1846), *abolitionize* (1854), *abolitioner* (1855), *abolitiondom* (1857), and *abolitionary* (1859). The most important of these was *abolitionize*, 'to imbue with the principles of the abolitionists' in order

2275.57 R 2

to effect the abolition of slavery. 'The Know Nothings have abolitionized Pennsylvania' is a sentence which might well puzzle the English reader unacquainted with American political history. Connected with this question are *Africanize* (1853) and *Africanization* (1856), mentioned by Bartlett in 1859 as 'words of recent introduction by Southern political writers', and used to denote or suggest the placing of the southern States under negro domination as the result of emancipation. 'This is a white man's country, and a white man's government, and the white race will never allow a section of it to be Africanized' is a typical example of the use of the verb. To designate the American negro the new compounds *Africo-American* and *Afro-American* appear in 1835 and 1890 respectively. The mixture of the white and black races having been denoted by *amalgamation* (p. 214),[1] naturally gave rise to *amalgamationist*, one who favoured such a union, a name which Harriet Martineau recorded as applied to her in 1838 ('I told her that the party term was new to me'), and the rarer *amalgamator* (1865). That *Americanize* should be of domestic origin was only natural, and its very beginning appears in 1797: 'I wish to see our people more Americanized, if I may use that expression; until we feel and act as an independent nation, we shall always suffer from foreign intrigue' (J. Jay *Corr. and P.* IV. 232). As in this example, the transitive use (frequently in the past participle) has been common from the first years of the nineteenth century; the intransitive also from 1875, 'he was Americanizing in that good lady's hands as fast as she could transform him'. Along with this go *Americanization* and *Americanizing*, both from 1858 onwards. *Anglify*, used by Franklin in 1751 and by succeeding writers, anticipates the English use by more than sixty years, and the Scottish *Englify* by well over seventy. 'Why should Pennsylvania', Franklin wrote, 'become a colony of aliens, who will shortly be so numerous as to Germanize us instead of our Anglifying them.' The idea of 'Americanizing' the immigrant had not yet arisen. To distinguish an American of English descent from one belonging to other races the compound *Anglo-American* was introduced and in common use from 1787. A little earlier (1781-2) it had

---

[1] References so given are to the pages of Tract No. LVI containing the first part of this study, or to those of this second part.

been applied by Jefferson to the Canadians on account of their continued adherence to England, but this limitation failed to maintain itself. 'The greater part [of the white inhabitants of the United States] are descended from the English, and, for the sake of distinction, are called Anglo-Americans' (1797 Morse *Amer. Geog.* 63). In the south, at a later date (1834–), the term was used by way of contrast to those of French or Spanish origin: 'a clothing or hat-store, kept by Americans, that is to say, Anglo-Americans as distinguished from the Louisianian French' (1835). The adjective *Anglo-American* (anticipated by the French *anglo-américain* of 1784) was also in common use from 1809 with such nouns as colonization, colony, civilization, race, &c., with the same connotation as the noun, more rarely to indicate independent connexion of England and America, as in 'an Anglo-American publishing house'. Minor examples of the same type of compound are *Anglo-Yankee* (1846); also *Anglo-federal* (1800), *Anglo-confederate* (1864), and *Anglo-rebel* (1864), these three indicating a leaning towards England or acting in concert with it. Excessive admiration for, or attachment to, England account for *Angloman* (1787), *Anglomania* (1787), and *Anglomany* (1793), all three used by Jefferson. The first two of these anticipate English instances, but Carlyle's *Anglo-maniac* (1837) has not been noted in American use before 1880. *Anglophobia* was also used by Jefferson in 1793 (in England by W. Taylor in 1816), and the adjective *Anglophobiac* appears a century later.

Americanism in its earliest sense was introduced by a Scot, Dr. John Witherspoon, who had been president of the College of New Jersey for fifteen years when in a series of articles on 'the present state of the English language in America' he made special mention of 'Americanisms, or ways of speaking peculiar to this country. . . . The word Americanism, which I have coined for the purpose, is exactly similar in its formation and signification to the word Scotticism.' In this sense, which had already become common in the United States, it was used by Miss Mitford in 1826: 'Society has been progressing (if I may borrow that expressive Americanism) at a very rapid rate.' Next in order comes the sense of 'adherence or attachment to America', 'a love of America and a preference of her interest' (Webster), beginning with Jefferson in 1797, followed by that of 'adoption or display of American ideas, habits, etc.; an American peculiarity of views or conduct', traceable from 1857 onwards. A good example of this use is Lowell's 'The earnest simplicity and unaffected Americanism of his character'.

The converse of an Americanism in speech was labelled a *Briticism* (1868–) or *Britishism* (1894); a publication of 1883 was 'a well-arranged handbook of Briticisms, Americanisms, Colloquial Phrases, etc.' A similar formation of an earlier date is *Britisher* (1829–), which is undoubtedly of American origin in spite of the desire of some American writers to disclaim it.

To American history belong *annexationist* (1852–), 'one who advocates the annexation of outside territory to the United States', and *Bourbonism* (1884–), 'obstinate conservatism in politics' (cf. p. 216) with the more recent *bourbonish* and *bourbonize*.

The followers of William Miller, who from 1831 preached the doctrine that Christ was coming again to establish a personal reign on earth, had received the name of *adventists* by 1844, and the doctrine itself that of *adventism* by 1874.

Some miscellaneous nouns denoting persons or things may be taken in order of date. *Abutter*, 'an owner of contiguous property or land', appearing in regular use from 1673 to the present time. *Bootee* (1799–), a boot covering the ankle but not the leg. *Bindery* (1810–), a bookbinder's establishment, possibly after the Dutch *binderij*, noted by the Penny Cyclopædia in 1833 as an Americanism and 'not a bad word'. *Book-bindery* (1815–) is also American. *Bakery* (1827–), also possibly from the Dutch *bakkerij*, noted as a novelty by English visitors to the United States as late as 1846: 'the signs were no less striking to a stranger. *Bakery* showed where one of life's great essentials could be bought.' This had passed into English use by 1857. Of the same type is *ashery* (1828–), a manufacturing plant for pearl-ash or potash. *Baseballist* (1868–), a player or supporter of baseball; also *baseballer* (1888), and *baseballism* (1870–), the pursuit of baseball, or an expression derived from baseball; 'there are the men who bunch their hits, to use a baseballism'. *Bicycler* (1879–), appearing at the same date as *bicyclist*, the latter having an English precedence of a few years.

There are a few derivative adjectives to be noticed. *Brushy* (1658–), of land overgrown or covered with brush or brushwood; 'it being brushy or bushy land we opened it by cutting away the bushes', 'high land thickly timbered, brushy, and almost impossible to penetrate'. *Boatable* (1683–), navigable by boat; 'the Susquehannah is navigable, or, as the Americans say, *boatable*, down the stream, nearly from its rise', was noted by an English traveller before 1800. *Breachy* (1780–), of horses, cattle, or sheep, apt to break through fences, 'a common word among the farmers of New England' says Pickering in 1813. *Brainy* (1874), provided with good brains, possessing intellectual ability; 'a fresh, brainy, courageous, forceful man'. *Amendatory* (1790–), of the nature of an amendment, as in 'amendatory act', 'amendatory bill', 'articles amendatory to the Constitution of the United States'. *Associational* (1815–), pertaining to an association of churches or clergymen, as in 'associational meeting', 'associational district', 'the associational or presbyterial examination'. *Appointive* (1881–), of a post or office, suitable for being filled by appointment, 'high appointive posts under the federal government'.

The participial *alkalied* (1864–) denotes either impregnated with alkali or affected by living in an alkali region (p. 206); 'you're so plumb alkalied you don't know the real thing when you see it'. The verb *burglarize* (1871–) has been used in several senses, especially in that of 'to rob (a house, &c.) as a burglar', as in 'a case where the post-office was burglarized'.

2

Far more numerous than the new derivatives or compounds are the attributive and adjectival collocations which have been steadily added to the American vocabulary, especially during the nineteenth century. The majority of these are perfectly natural combinations, which might as readily have come into English use if they had been required. This, however, does not remove them from the category of true Americanisms, since their origin and currency have been due to conditions and circumstances not prevailing in England. An American reviewer of the first two parts of the Dictionary of American English objected to the inclusion of such combinations as *bear-trap*. 'It may be true', he argued, 'that the earliest known quotations for *bear-trap* are American, but the formation is characteristic of the English language, and sure to appear whenever one has occasion to set traps for bears. The compound *bear-trap* is in itself no more American than *mouse-trap*.' No doubt, if considered abstractly as examples of compound terms, *bear-trap* and *mouse-trap* belong to the same category, but it is obvious that the complete absence of wild bears in England during the historic period gave no occasion for the use of *bear-trap*, whereas it was natural, and even necessary, for the American pioneer. To deny the American claim to any collocation which *could* also originate in English would exclude from the dictionary hundreds of its most characteristic entries. Even the accidental occurrence in English of some of these collocations is not sufficient to outweigh the fact that in regular use they are distinctively American.

Among terms connected with civil or military life are the following. *Artillery sermon* (1644–), a sermon preached on the day of the *artillery election* (1673–), i.e. the election of the Artillery Company of Boston. This appears under that name in 1650, thirty years earlier than the first recorded English example, but it would be hazardous to assume American priority without further inquiry.

Interest in the abolition of slavery (cf. p. 225) led to the founding of the *Abolition Society* of Pennsylvania (1790–), followed by others in the first half of the following century. The *abolition party* is mentioned as existent from 1852 to 1863. The special sense of *appropriation* (p. 213) gave rise to *appropriation bill*, a legislative bill proposing or authorizing a particular application of money, in regular use from 1789. *Auction* enters into several combinations not current in English, as *auction store* (1785–); *auction duty* (1827–53), a duty levied on sales by auction; *auction house* (1848–), a firm of auctioneers; *auction stand* (1846–8) and *auction block* (1860–73), both applied to the stand or block on which a slave stood when put up to auction. That *auction sale* (1820–) is recorded much earlier than in English use (1898) is probably accidental, although the usual English phrase is 'sale by auction'. The *annuity* (p. 215) paid to Indian tribes provides various combinations, as *annuity money* (1849–), *annuity Indian* (1870), and

especially *annuity goods* (1868–).   From *army* are formed
army register (1815–), the counterpart of the British 'army
list'; *army wagon* (1865–) and *army blue* (1881–), the blue
uniform formerly worn by the United States or the Federal
army. The English dictionaries do not enable comparative
dates to be given for *army corps* and *army regulations*, both
current in the U.S. from 1847.   In 1840 'the ladies of
New Orleans . . . offered a splendid banner to the State
which should give the largest relative majority for Harrison
and Tyler in its popular vote for Presidential Electors'.
Hence in the same year came the designations of *Banner
State* and *Banner County*, which led the way to a general
use of the word to express supreme excellence or standing,
as *banner veteran* (1853), *banner town* (1882), *banner crop*
(1886), *banner claim* (in mining), &c.   Misuse of the
ballot as a method of voting is disclosed in *ballot-box stuffer*
and *stuffing* (1856–); the latter is described by Bartlett in
1859 as 'a new name for a new crime. This consists in the
use of a box for receiving ballots at an election, so con-
structed with a false bottom and compartments as to permit
the introduction of spurious ballots to any extent by the
party having it in charge.' By 1888, however, it was 'an
almost obsolete form in New York under its election system'.   *Blockade*, in addition to *blockade runner* and *running*
(p. 221), furnished *blockade whisky* (1883) as a name for
illicit whisky, mentioned earlier (1867) simply as *blockade*,
and *blockade tobacco* (1886).
   Book-account (1672–1883), though not recorded in English
use, may well have been current there, but various combinations of *book* are clearly American. The earliest of these is
book-store, common from 1763 to the present day. Others
are *book-bindery* (p. 228), *book concern* (1844–), an establishment engaged in publishing or selling books, *book-peddler*
(1844–), *book-agent* (1848–); also with different connotation
in *book-farmer* (1849–), one who farms from books instead
of, or in addition to, experience, and *book-farming* (1854–).
From about 1830 attributive uses of *business* appear to
have been more common in the United States than in
England, and priority in date may reasonably be claimed
for a number of these, even if they are now equally current
in English use. Such are *business man* (1832–), *business
woman* (1844–), *business agent* (1849–), *business manager*

(1865-); *business letter* (1844-), *business centre* (1851-), *business college* (1877-), *business office* (1877-), *business street* (1881-), and the adjective *business-like* (1860-).

Bible class (1824-) appears to be of American origin, which is clearly to be assigned to *Bible Christian* (*c.* 1819-), 'a sect closely resembling the Methodists', and *Bible Communist* (1867-), a member of a sect founded by the social reformer J. H. Noyes. Religion and philanthropy are also represented by *Amen Corner* (1860-), 'the part of a church occupied by those who have a habit of expressing assent during the service', and *aid society* (1853-), an organization, commonly of ladies, engaged in rendering various kinds of assistance, frequently with defining additions, as *children's, emigrants', soldiers' aid society.*

In addition to the derivatives mentioned above (p. 228), *baseball* provides *baseball club* (1855-), a club of baseball players, and (1884-) the bat used in playing the game, *baseball match* (1856-), and *baseball player* (1859-), as well as *baseball bat, game, ground, nine, team,* &c. From *base,* one of the several stations of the baseball ground, are formed *base-bag* (1867-), *base-player* (1867-), *base-runner* (1867-), *base-playing* (1868-), *base-running* (1886-), *base-stealing* (1891-), &c. *Basket ball* was invented and named by James Naismith in 1891. An earlier combination of the same word was *basket meeting,* defined by Bartlett in 1859 as 'in the West, a sort of picnic, generally with some religious exercises'. A full account from 1892 states that 'Basket meetings are not confined to the Southern negroes. On the contrary they are more common among the white people. Neither are they always religious. Quite frequently they are political, sometimes educational.'

Travel or transport by land or water provide some new terms. *Boating,* which at an early date (1660-) acquired the practical sense of transporting by boat ('by the canal, it would cost in boating fifteen cents, for 300 miles'), accounts for *boating place* (1637) and *boating business* (1755). The importance of boats for river traffic becomes obvious in the nineteenth century in such combinations as *boat yard* (1805-), *boat water* (1804), water navigable by boats, *boat canal* (1813-), *boat landing* (1826-), *boat hand* (1821-), *boat stores* (1835-41), *boat horn* (1835-), a horn used by river boatman for signalling, and *boat corn* (1849), corn taken

south by boat, especially from Ohio and Kentucky.   A
coach or train which made stops on the route to take up or
set down passengers was distinguished as an *accommodation
stage* (1811–60), *coach* (1830–40), *car* (1836), or *train*
(1838–), and the usage was extended to *accommodation line*
(1834) and *fare* (1811). By a natural ellipse *accommodation*
by itself was used to denote the coach or train (p. 213).

A direct (or nearly direct) line between two places was
known as an *air-line* from 1813, and this subsequently
(1853–) came to be applied to a railway carried in a straight
line, as on the prairies, or in the most direct line between
two points, sometimes also more fully called an *air-line railroad* or *railway*. Although used by Grote in 1852 *air-line*
has not established itself in English, while the synonymous
bee-line (1830–) has been accepted without reserve. The
reason for the latter term is concisely expressed by a writer
of 1848: 'when the bee has sucked its fill, it rises, makes
two or three circuits, and then moves off in a straight, a
"bee-line", to the swarm of which it is a member.'   A
different sense of *air* attaches to *air-town* (1880), a town
which is still 'in the air' and yet to be built, like the synonymous 'lithograph town'.

Baggage, which in the United States has taken the place
of the British *luggage*, enters into a surprising number of
attributive collocations, largely due to the methods of
handling baggage on the American railways, which make
these combinations more natural or necessary than their
counterparts would be in Britain. Such are *baggage car*
(1835), *baggage room* (1831–), *baggage crate* (1839–), *baggage
check* (1854–), *baggage express* (1859–), *baggage coach* (1878–),
baggage rack (1889), &c., and the personal designations
baggage agent (1858–), *baggage man* (1863–), *baggage clerk*
(1870–), *baggage expressman* (1872–). The sarcastic *baggage-
smasher* (1856–) has been a favourite designation of one who
handles baggage at a dock or railway station, 'so called from
the reckless manner in which these persons handle the
property of travellers' (Bartlett), and the verbal noun *baggage-
smashing* is recognized by the laws of Illinois in 1883 in
providing penalties for 'any person employed by a railroad
corporation in this state, who shall wilfully, carelessly or
negligently break, injure, or destroy any baggage'.

A typically American vehicle is the *bob-sled* (1848–), a

sled having two pairs of short runners, 'prepared for the transport of large timber from the forest to a river or public road' (Bartlett); also (1890–), 'a sled for coasting made of two pairs of runners connected by a long board'. In the latter sense *bob-sleigh* (1889–) is also in use.

It may be accidental that *bridle-way* (1703–) and *bridle-road* (1775–) are recorded earlier in American than in English use (1760 and 1833 respectively), but *bridle-track* (1837–) has a fair chance of being purely American, in contrast to *bridle-path*, of which the earliest English example (1811) antedates the American (1833).

Alleyway as a synonym of *alley* has been current since 1788, and is also (1854–) applied to a narrow passage-way in a building or on board a steamship; 'Cynthia entered the other stateroom and shut the door to the alleyway'. More recently (1903–) *areaway* has been introduced to denote a sunk area serving as a passage-way; 'the building is connected with the main hospital by a covered areaway'.

The verbal noun *building* enters into various combinations which are distinctively American, as *building lot* (1701–); *building yard* (1701–), for boat-building or ship-building; *building rock* (1800–49) = building stone; *building paper* (1873–), a thick paper used by builders as a covering or lining material. Of doubtful priority, as full evidence on the English side is not available, are *building timber* (1647–), *building stone* (1790–), and *building association* (1851–).

The *barn* (p. 207) had a prominent place in pioneer life, and has furnished a number of new combinations, as *barn-room* (1639–), 'barn room for his corn', 'barn room for keeping a cow'; *barn-plot* (1676–); *barn-lot* (1724–); *barn-chamber* (1838–), a loft above a barn; *barn-grass* (1821–) = barn-yard grass (see below); *barn-ball* (1850–), 'which means throwing a ball at the gable and catching it when it returns'; *barn-dance* (1855–), a dance held in a barn, 'but ... it is difficult to see why the title is specially applied to this Scotch lilt and schottische hops'. *Barn-raising* (1856–), like *house-raising*, implies the co-operation of neighbours and the social gathering on this occasion. The political term *barn-burner* (1845–, but originating in 1842–3) was applied to 'a member of the more progressive section of the Democratic party', and had the accompanying adjective *barn-burning* (c. 1848). The use of barns by itinerant actors

gave rise to *barn-stormer* and *barn-storming* (1884–), and to
the verb *barn-storm* (1896) in an extended sense: 'he was
barn-storming down in Georgia in favour of gold mono-
metallism.' *Barn-swallow* (1790–) may prove to have been
in English use before the earliest recorded instance of 1851.
Barn-yard, common in older Scottish (15th–17th cent.) and
locally known in England, has had full currency in American use from the seventeenth century, and is also common
in *barn-yard manure* (1819–), *barn-yard fowl* (1843–; Eng.
barn-door fowl, c. 1685–), and *barn-yard grass* (1843–), usually
a synonym of cockspur grass.

   Bathing-house (1760–), as an alternative for *bath-house*
(1800–; Eng. from 1705) and *bathing-room* for *bath-room*
(1836–; Eng. from 1780) appear to be Americanisms.
Boarding-house (1787–) may not be American, though not
recorded in English before 1823, but *boarding-place* (1854–)
and *boarding-hall* (1868–) may safely be assigned to the
United States.   American origin is also clear in *apartment
house* (1876–), *apartment building* (1876–) and *apartment
hotel* (1902–); for this use of 'apartment' see p. 215.   'The
bar-room of a public house is what in England is called a
tap-room' was written by an English traveller in 1809. This
has been in regular use from 1807, and occurs freely in
attributive combinations as *bar-room table, counter, floor,
window,* &c.   From the same noun comes *bar-tender* (1855–)
for a barman or bar-keeper.

   A frame for a building having light wooden uprights
secured by simple nailing had acquired the name of a
balloon-frame by 1853, and a house so built is a *balloon-
frame house* (1873–83), *balloon house* (1855), or simply a
balloon (1855).   Another combination of 'house' is *bough-
house* (1811–), a temporary structure made of boughs serving as a blind in wild-fowl shooting or as a shelter in
camping out; 'down in the bough-house the campers re-
clined in comfortable attitudes'.

   Division of land in the early settlements being a matter
of importance accounts for a number of combinations with
bound as their first element, viz. *bound-stake* (1655–), *bound-
tree* (1663–), *bound-line* (1664–), *bound house* (1665–), and
bound-corner (1670–). Although *bound-mark* (1640–) is found
earlier in England (1623), yet it clearly had greater currency
in the colonies down to at least 1735. *Boundary line* (1705–)

was common in American use long before its first record in
English (1842).

Border, coming to be applied specially to the Western
frontier, is frequent after 1830 in attributive uses which
are purely and naturally American, as *border Indians, tribe,
settlers, ranchmen, prairie*, &c., and provides certain fixed
combinations such as *border war* (1809–), *border warfare*
(1835–), *border life* (1827–), *border State* (1849–), and the
more distinctive *Border ruffian* (1856–), one of the pro-
slavery party in Missouri who in 1854–8 made incursions
into Kansas to outvote or intimidate the anti-slavery party
there, their practices or conduct being designated *border-
ruffianism* (1861–).

The inhabitants or natives of various bays on the Atlantic
coast, and especially those of the colony of Massachusetts
Bay, have been known as *baymen* from 1641; a later and less
lasting application of the term was to the mahogany cutters
of the Bay of Honduras (1715–).   The use of *bottom* to
denote low-lying land along a river or stream, formerly
current in England, has remained in full use in America,
and has given rise to such attributive combinations of a
permanent nature as *bottom ground* (1637–), *bottom land*
(1728–), *bottom prairie* (1807–), *bottom timber* (1837–), *bottom grass* (1850), together with many of lesser currency, as
bottom plain, lot, tract, soil, field, farmer, people, &c.   *Bog*,
with a slightly different connotation from that usual in
English, enters into *bog meadow* (1749–), *bog plough* (1748),
bog hoe (1854), *bog mouse* (1857), *bog birch* (1897), and is
especially frequent with names of plants, as *bog evergreen*
(1784), *bog gale* (1785), *bog moss* (1791–), *bog potato* (1800),
bog grass (1821–), *bog onion* (1832–), and *bog sedge* (1840–).
Branch, in its new sense of 'stream' (p. 205) has given *branch
swamp* (1832–) and *branch water* (1866–).   *Bench* in its
topographical sense (p. 205) has supplied *bench-land* (1857–;
'the entire valley, with all the bench-lands and the mountains surrounding these') and *bench-bottom* (1867; 'the second
or bench-bottoms on the Missouri').

The substitution of 'meeting-house' for 'church' sufficiently explains the replacing of 'churchyard' by *burying
yard* (1698–) as a synonym of the earlier (also English)
burying place and later *burying ground* (1759–; also English
from 1711). *Burying lot* (1882) is obviously American. A

slang equivalent is *bone-yard* (1872–), as in 'You or me'll
have to go to the boneyard', by transference from the earlier
sense (1862–) of that word, viz. a place where the bones of
dead animals are collected for subsequent use.

The names of native trees appear in various combinations,
as *alder-swamp* (1640–), *ash-swamp* (1668–), and *birch-swamp*
(1660–); 'one species [of tree] generally predominating in
each soil has originated the descriptive names of maple, ash,
and cedar swamps'.   The use made of the bark of the birch-
tree naturally led to the early currency of *birch-bark* (1643–),
as well as combinations of this, as *birch-bark cradle, hut,* &c.,
and especially *birch-bark canoe* (1805–) for the earlier *birch-
canoe* (*c.* 1649) and *birchen canoe* (1634).   *Bush* enters into
various types of combinations, as *bush lot* (1694), *bush pasture*
(1817–), *bush arbor* (1848–), *bush country* (1855), *bush field*
(1857), *bush land* (1867); *bush-hook* (1834–) and *bush-scythe*
(1856–; perhaps a new formation though used by Huloet
in 1552); *bush clover* (1817–), *bush honeysuckle* (1817–), *bush
bean* (1836–); *bush rat* (1867–), *bush sparrow* (1858), and
bush titmouse (1881–).   *Bushloper* (1694–1752) was an adap-
tation of the Dutch *boschloper*, equivalent to the French
'coureur de bois'.   A novel term for a dweller in the backwoods was found in *bushwhacker* (1809–), which during the
Civil War acquired the specialized sense of one who carried
on guerrilla warfare in the woods. With this went *bushwhack-
ing* as an adjective (1813–) and a verbal noun with several
significations, including a political sense (1841–); 'all he
asked for was a clear field and fair fight—no *bush-whacking*,
if he might be indulged in an expressive word, well under-
stood in the border wars of the West'.   The verb *bushwhack*
also appears in 1836, and is current in various senses after
1860.   A widely different sense attaches to *bush-meeting*
(1863–77), a religious meeting held in the woods, 'distinguished from *camp-meetings* in the fact of lasting only one
day (the Sabbath usually), having no tents put up, and being
in every respect more impromptu' (Bartlett).   The prevalence of brushwood in the new country not only led to the
retention of the older English *brush bill* and *brush scythe*,
but gave occasion for the introduction of a number of new
combinations, as *brush plain* (1684), *brush fence* (1729–),
brush camp (1776–), *brush land* (1853), *brush house* (1862),
brush hut (1889), and *brush whiskey* (1885–), 'that important

beverage, variously known as "blockade", "brush whiskey", and in the outer world as "corn-whiskey", which is extracted from the grain and surreptitiously distributed'. Parallel formations to some of these are *briar scythe* (1813–), *briar-hook* (1819–), and *briar patch* (*c.* 1845–).

The extensive cultivation of the apple in America is illustrated by a surprising number of new combinations. *Apple orchard* (1721–) is earlier than in the English record by over eighty years. Among the articles of food or drink made from the fruit are *apple brandy* (*c.* 1780–), *apple toddy* (1809–), *apple jack* (1816–), *apple butter* (1819–), *apple slump* (1831–), and *apple leather* (1877–); some of these require explanation to the outsider. Social gatherings for dealing with the fruit by way of preserving it are variously named *apple-paring* (1819–), *apple-bee* (1827–), *apple-cut* (1845–), *apple-cutting* (1850–), and *apple-peeling* (1871–). An *apple-roaster* is mentioned as early as 1642, *apple-parer* in 1833, and *apple-peeler* in 1858. In the nineteenth century various insects or grubs attacking the apple-tree have received the names of *apple-beetle* (1832–), *apple-bug* (1832–), *apple-worm* (1850–), *apple-borer* (1858), *apple-tree borer* (1838), *apple-twig borer* (1850–), *apple-maggot* (1867), and *apple-codling* (1871). Of the combinations of *bean* some are plainly American as *bean-vine* (1828–), *bean-patch* (1850), *bean-pot* (1829), *bean-shooter* (1889–), the counterpart of a pea-shooter, and *bean-weevil* (1870–). Others, as *bean-pole* (1821–), *bean-porridge* (1828–), and *bean-soup* (1837–), have at least a clearer American record according to the present evidence. The abundance of wild berries (blueberries, cranberries, huckleberries) in some parts gives rise to a number of combinations not required in England, as *berry-lot* (1845), *berry-field* (1855–), *berry pasture* (1880–), *berry-patch* (1896–); *berry-picker* (1867–), *berry-picking* (1885–), *berry party* (1860), *berry season* (1875–); *berry pie* (1876); *berry moth* (1884). Similar combinations occur in *blueberry swamp* (1828), *blueberry patch* (1887), *blueberry flat* (1895), *blueberry land* and *blueberry plain* (1902).

Buckwheat being more extensively cultivated in the United States than in England gives rise to *buckwheat field* (1799), *buckwheat stubble* (1835), *buckwheat meadow*, *buckwheat patch* (1887); *buckwheat cake* (1774–), for which the simple *buckwheat* is also (1830–) used, 'another plate of hot buckwheats'; *buckwheat meal* (1768–) and *buckwheat flour* (1805–). Transferred uses appear in *buckwheat tree* (1813–), a tall Southern evergreen ; *buckwheat nose* (1842), the hog-nosed or blowing snake; and *buckwheat coal* (1881–), the smallest grade of coal sent to market.

Arbor Day is a purely American institution, being a day 'named by law, and also by custom, for planting forest trees to make lumber for the generations yet to come'. The observance was initiated in Nebraska in April 1872.

Among new names of trees or plants are several combinations of *box*, as *boxberry* (1706–), the checkerberry or winter-green, and the fruit of this; *box oak* (1785–) and *box white oak* (1810–); *box elder* (1787–) and *box alder* (1805–), the ash-leaved maple.   *Arrow-wood* (1709–), applied to several shrubs or small trees bearing slender straight shoots or branches suitable for making arrows.   *Bow-wood* (1806–), the Osage orange or yellow wood, known also by the French name *bois d'arc* (1805), Americanized as *bowdark* (1844) and *bodock* (1847–).   *Butternut* (1741–), the white wal-nut, also (1753–) the nut borne by this, (1820–) the wood or bark of the tree, or the hull of the nut, and (1810–) the colour obtained by using the bark, roots, &c., as a dye. The tree itself is also called *butternut tree* (1770–). Attri-butive uses mainly denote the colour derived from the nut, as *butternut suit* (1859–), *butternut jeans* (1867), *butternut homespun*, &c.; also the adj. *butternut-coloured* (1830–). A *butternut* was also the name given to a Confederate soldier in the Civil War or to a Northerner whose sympathies were with the South at that time.   *Buck-eye* (1763–), one or other species of American horse-chestnut, 'so called on account of the resemblance which its darkbrown nut bears to a buck's eye, when the shell first cracks and exposes it to sight' (Clapin). The natural application of the name to the nut itself is later (1817–) and rarer; greater currency attaches to the transferred sense of a native or inhabitant of a backwoods region (1823–), in later use specifically of Ohio, which has thus acquired the name of the *Buck-eye State* (1840–).

The usefulness of certain plants or trees for making brooms accounts for *broom corn* (1781–), a species of millet, *broom straw* (1785–), *broom grass* (1793–), *broom sedge* (1819–); *broom pine* (1791–), *broom birch* (1810–), *broom hickory* (1813), and *broom brush* (1888–), a species of St. John's wort.

Several of the larger animals, and some of the smaller forms of animal life, enter freely into combinations natural in the new surroundings. The absence of the beaver in England sufficiently accounts for only one combination, *beaver hat*, being known before 1600. On the other hand, the prevalence of the animal in America, and the value of its fur, gave rise to a whole series of attributive formations relating to it in its various aspects. The pelt and its uses are represented by *beaver skin* (1616–) and *beaver fur* (1747–), *beaver coat* (1634–) and *beaver coating* (1759–), *beaver blanket* (1752–) and *beaver robe* (1791–), and its commercial value by *beaver pay* or *beaver price* (1662–), and *beaver trade* (1632–). The homes of the beaver supplied *beaver pond* (1640–), *beaver meadow* (1644–), *beaver dam* (1660–), *beaver house* (1765–), *beaver lodge* (1805–), *beaver stream* (1837–), and *beaver canal* (1868–). A *beaver country* (1761–1837) was one in which beaver abounded. The catching of beaver provided *beaver-hunter* (1687–), *beaver-hunting* (1722–), *beaver hunt* (1848); also *beaver trap* (1709–), *beaver-trapper* (1819–), and *beaver-trapping* (1823). Indications of the presence of beaver gave *beaver-sign* (1822–). Among other types of combinations are *beaver tree* (1753–), the sweet magnolia or bay-tree; *beaver-wood* (1810–), the bay-tree or (1813–) the hackberry; *beaver-eater* (1771–), the wolverine, and *beaver (field-) mouse* (1842). In all no less than forty-five such combinations of *beaver* form separate entries in the dictionary.

Another notable wild animal, the bear, presented various features requiring new combinations to designate them. From the animal could be obtained *bearskin* (1647–, in common use in the 18th century, but rare in Eng. before 1800), *bear's oil* (1674–), *bear's fat* (1709–, also *bear-fat*, 1780–), *bear's meat* (1772–, also *bear-meat* 1787–), *bear-bacon* (1772–), *bear-steak* (1788–), and *bear-chowder* (1847). To the hunting of the bear belong *bear-hunting* (1705–), *bear-hunter* (1765–), *bear-hunt* (1803–), *bear-trap* (1825–), and *bear-sign* (1839–); a curious application of the latter is to a doughnut (1903). Miscellaneous examples are *bear-dance*, among the Indians (*a.* 1820–); *bear-grass* (1750–), a species of yucca, also the camas or quamash; *bear-ground* (1797–);

bear-oak (1810–), the black scrub oak; *Bear State* (1848), Arkansas and (1872) California; *bear-tree* (1808–), a tree in which a bear lies concealed during the winter; *bear-wallow* (1843–), a shallow depression attributed to the wallowing of bears. In all, the dictionary makes separate entry of thirty-six such combinations.

The buck or male deer enters into several combinations in common use. *Buckshot* is first mentioned in 1775[1] in connexion with an engagement between the American riflemen and the British troops: 'The reason that so many more of the King's troops were wounded than killed ... is that the Americans use a small shot, called buck-shot, which is much smaller than the soldiers' bullets.' (On the abbreviation of this to *buck*, and other uses of the monosyllable, see p. 208.) *Bucktail* (1821–, and *buck's tail* 1775–1836), in addition to its literal sense, has been applied (1818–) to a member of the Tammany Society in New York and in the plural (1862–) to a regiment of Pennsylvania troops in the Civil War, more fully called the *Bucktail Rifles*. To these may be added *buck-handled* (1840–), having a handle made of buck-horn; *buck fever* (1841–) and *buck ague* (1844), the nervous excitement felt by a novice in hunting at the sight of a deer; and *buck brush* (1874–), bushes or shrubs on which deer feed. The sense of 'male' appears in *buck elk* (1750–) and as applied to persons in *buck Indian* (1840–) and *buck negro* or *nigger* (1853–).

Along with the beaver and the bear, one of the most distinctive animals of the new country was the buffalo (p. 208), the importance of which is shown by the number of combinations into which it enters, all of them naturally of American origin. A fair number of these occur before 1800, but the majority appear first in the nineteenth century, after the region west of the Mississippi, with its immense herds of buffaloes, became better known. From the country inhabited or traversed by the buffalo comes a long series of attributive uses, viz. *buffalo range* (1775–), *buffalo plain* (1781–), *buffalo country* (1833–), *buffalo ground* (1837–), *buffalo region* (1848–), *buffalo run* (1867–); *buffalo road* (1750–), *buffalo path* (1770–), *buffalo crossing* (1775–), *buffalo beat* (1805–), *buffalo track* (1806–), *buffalo trace*

---

[1] An apparent example from 1447–8 cited in the O.E.D. is clearly an error for *but* (i.e. butt) *shot*.

(1823–), *buffalo trail* (c. 1834), *buffalo ford* (1836–), *buffalo street* (1837–); *buffalo lick* (1780–), *buffalo wallow* (1834–), *buffalo stamp* (1873–). Next to these in point of number are those denoting parts of the animal or articles obtained from it, as *buffalo skin* (1732–), *buffalo hide* (1800–); *buffalo steak* (1770–), *buffalo beef* (1775–), *buffalo meat* (1779–), *buffalo tongue* (1792–), *buffalo hump* (1827–), *buffalo tallow* (1805); *buffalo horn* (1783–), *buffalo wool* (1814–). From the hide came *buffalo robe* (1804–; cf. p. 208), *buffalo rug* (1805–), *buffalo coat* (1845), and *buffalo wrapper* (1846); also *buffalo tug* (1832–), a thong of buffalo hide, and *buffalo boat* (1844–), one made 'by stretching the hide of those animals over a frame of poles, or, what is still more common, over an empty wagon-body'. The sex and age were naturally denoted by *buffalo bull* (1821–), *buffalo cow* (1779–), and *buffalo calf* (1775–, with *buffalo calf-skin*, 1847–). From the chase of the buffalo came *buffalo-hunt* (1808–), *buffalo hunting* (1821–), and *buffalo-hunter* (1843–), *buffalo sign* (1805–), *buffalo horse* (1832–), and *buffalo runner* (a. 1849–), both denoting horses used or trained for the hunt; 'the Sioux have stolen more than four hundred horses, many of them buffalo runners'. The *buffalo dance* (1805–) was performed by the Indians 'to cause the buffalo to come near so that they may kill them'. *Buffalo chips* (1840–) was the name given to dried pieces of buffalo dung used as fuel on the prairies.

Various fishes and insects are distinguished by having this name prefixed, as the *buffalo fish* (1781–), *buffalo carp* (1820), *buffalo pike* (1842), *buffalo perch* (1845), and *buffalo cod* (1890); *buffalo gnat* (1822–), *buffalo fly* (1846–), *buffalo bug* (1889), *buffalo beetle* (1889), and *buffalo moth* (1892). The common grey wolf of the western plains is also known as the *buffalo wolf* (1846–). Several plants and bushes, or their fruit, also have this epithet, as *buffalo grass* (1784–), *buffalo clover* (1785–), *buffalo berry* (1805–, whence *buffalo berrying* 1882), *buffalo bush* (1833–), *buffalo nut* (1857–), *buffalo currant* (1863–), *buffalo tree* (1883–), and *buffalo bur* (1894).

In all, seventy-eight such combinations are dealt with as separate entries in the dictionary, while thirty-eight more are given by way of subordinate examples.

The bull, both domesticated and wild, has also furnished

a large number of combinations; in some of these it is used where the normal English would be 'bullock' or 'ox'. Bull denotes the male animal in *bull buffalo* (1750–), *bull moose* (1839–), *bull elk* (1886–), and a male person in *bull nigger* (1825–40; cf. *buck nigger* above). The driving of cattle or the use of oxen account for *bull-whacker* (1859–) with *bull-whacking* (1870) and the verb *bull-whack* (1896–), *bull-puncher* (1874–), and *bull-driver* (1877–); *bull-train* (1864–), *bull-team* (1879–), and *bull-whip* (1852–). Miscellaneous uses are *bull-pen*, an enclosure for bulls, recorded as a place-name in 1823, but earlier (1809–) as a make-shift prison in the nature of a pen; 'when the jails would hold no more, they kept some hundred in an open stockade, called a bull-pen'. Also *bull-tongue plough* (1849–), or simply *bull-tongue* (1860–; also used as a verb); *bull-strong* (1873–) of a fence, strong enough to hold back a bull; 'a fence here, according to a saying of the section, must be "mule-high, bull-strong, and pig-tight"'. The buffalo is the animal implied in *bull-boat* (1832–; cf. *buffalo boat* above), *bull-dance* (1833), *bull-hole* (1837–), *bull-fever* (1839), *bull-meat* (1843–), and *bull-chip* (1870). Obscurity attaches to the origin of the verb *bulldoze* (1876–), to intimidate by violence or threats, especially for political purposes, with *bull-dozing* and *bull-dozer* from the same date. Of the few animals coming under this head the earliest is the *bull-frog* (1698–), 'which makes a roaring noise, hardly to be distinguished from that well known of the beast from whom it takes its name'. Others are *bull-neck* (1709–43), a sea-bird, *bull-snake* (1784–), *bull-pout* (1823–), *bull plover* (1844), and *bull-bat* (1851–). A dozen or more names of plants or fruits appear first in the nineteenth century, as *bull-grape* (1847–), *bull-sap* (1851–), *bull-brier* (1853–), *bull-nut* (1859–), *bull-berry* (1861–), *bull-thistle* (1863–), *bull-nettle* (1876–), *bull-bay* (1883), *bull-pine* (1884–), *bull-weed* (1884), *bull grass* (1894–).

The alligator, living in an *alligator hole* (1797–), lends its name to some other inhabitants of the water, as the *alligator fish* (1772–), *alligator gar* (1832–), *alligator terrapin* (1838–), *tortoise* (1839), or *turtle* (1839–), and *alligator snapper* (1884). *Alligator skin* (1820–), *tail* (1844–), and *hide* (1883–) are those of the animal itself, but an *alligator tooth* (1856) was a special form of tine on an implement for levelling ground.

Among new names for aquatic animals or fishes are *box turtle* (1833–) or *tortoise* (1839–), *box oyster* (1881) and *box crab* (1889); *bone fish* (1734–), *bone-shark* (1802–), and *bill-fish* (1782–).

The bee, though not indigenous to America, has made several distinctive additions to the vocabulary. *Bee-hunter* had been used incidentally in English (in an account of South Africa) in 1776, but from 1824 is current American, along with *bee-hunting* (1824–) and *bee-hunt* (1837–). The *bee-tree* (1782–) in which wild bees have their hive is frequently a gum-tree, a *bee-gum* (1817–), in the South and West; this also denotes a section of the hollow trunk of a gum-tree used as a hive (1848–), and so becomes an ordinary word for 'hive'; 'neither are there "hives" in the mountains, only "bee-gums", which the bees fill with "right smart of honey"'. The use of *bee-line* (1830–) to denote the direct line taken by a bee returning to its hive has already been mentioned in connexion with *air-line* (p. 233). The *bee-moth* infesting hives has been so called since 1829. Plant-names are *bee-balm* (1847–), and *bee-harvest* (a. 1847), the ox-eye daisy. *Bee-culture* (1856–) provides a more popular term than 'apiculture', and *bee-ranch* (1883–) is obviously American for bee-keeping on a large scale.

A long array of new combinations has been formed to serve as the distinctive names of material articles, the number and variety of which make it simplest to present them in alphabetical order; as the majority of them originate in the nineteenth century, the relative dating is of minor importance. The most noteworthy of these (including some others with the same first element) are the following:

Air-brake, a railway brake operated by compressed air, for which a patent was granted to G. Westinghouse in 1871. *Air-foundry* (1815–), one equipped with air furnaces (which are recorded in the United States in 1780 and in England in 1784). The adjective *air-tight* (Eng. 1760–) is used as a noun (1843–) by ellipse of 'stove'; 'she ran up stairs to build a fire in the little airtight'. *Ash-hopper* (1804–), *ash-box* (1846–), *ash-gum* (1851–), and *ash-barrel* (1870–), names of various receptacles for ashes. *Ash-cake* (1809–) and *ash-pone* (1816–), baked among or under hot ashes. *Axe-mark* (1832–), a mark cut on a tree with an axe; a blaze.

Bale-cloth (1797–) for covering bales, and *bale-rope* (1821–) for binding up bales, especially of cotton, the latter in very common use.   *Ball-ground* (1772– among the Indians; 1871– for baseball, &c.); *ball-stick* (1775–), the racket used by Indians in their ball-play, *ball-club*, either bat (1837–) or players (1845–); *ball-game* (1848–), *ball-team* (1888–), and *ball-park* (1899).   *Bark canoe* (1725–; cf. *birch-bark canoe*, p. 237), *bark hut* (1744–), and *bark-shanty* (1840). Also *bark-mill* (1749–), a mill for grinding bark for the use of tanners or dyers, and *bark-louse* (1841–), one infesting the bark of trees.   *Bar-share* (1785–) or *bar-shear* (1837–) *plough*, a plough having a bar extending backwards from the share, apparently an American invention.   *Base-board* (1853–), a skirting-board in a room, or a plank along the bottom of a fence.   *Base-burner* (1874–), a stove in which the fuel is fed automatically as the lower layer is consumed. Also *base-burner stove*, *base-burning furnace*. *Bath-tub* (1870–), for the earlier *bathing tub* (1832–), which occurs in English in 1583.   *Bed-rug* (1647–), *bed-covering* (c. 1656–), *bed-sack* (1661–), *bed-quilt* (1765–), *bed-clothing* (1852–); these, if not of American origin, have no corresponding record in English. In *bed-bunt* (1761–) and *bed-spread* (c. 1845–), the second element may be of Dutch or Low German origin.   *Bed-rock* (1850–), the solid rock underlying looser strata; frequently (1869–) in figurative uses, as 'we came down to bed-rock, as the miners say, i.e. an extra flannel shirt and a pocket comb'; 'they do not reach the hard-pan of wickedness, the bed-rock of depravity at once'.   *Bell* in *bell-button* (1775 and 1839–), in modern use, an ornamental button having the shape of a globular bell, *bell-crowned hat* (1821–) and *bell-crown* (1843–), *bell-cord* (1843–), and *bell-punch* (1877–) used by conductors in collecting fares. *Bell-horse* (1775–), *bell-mare* (1853–), and *bell-cow* (1878–) are of the same type as the English 'bell-wether'.   *Bill-board* (1851–), a board to which notices or posters are affixed. *Bill-head* (1845–), possibly as early in English but not recorded before 1879.   *Blanket* in *blanket bag* (1734–), *blanket coat* (1805–), *blanket capot* (1807–35), *blanket overcoat* (1822–), *blanket shawl* (1837–), and *blanket tent* (1852–). *Blanket sheet* (1870–), a large newspaper in folio form; 'the blanket sheets made their appearance in the city of New York in 1827'.   *Block-coal*

(1871–), a kind of coal readily mined in large blocks. *Blossom-rock* (1872–), for which the simple *blossom* (p. 211) is also used.   *Boiler deck* (1830–), the deck of a steamboat immediately above the boiler or boilers, 'the second story of the boat, so to speak' (Mark Twain). *Boiler iron* (1855–), iron suitable for making boilers, the equivalent of English *boiler-plate*, which in the United States (1893–) has acquired the sense of stereotyped matter issued to the newspaper press; 'the subsidizing of news agencies that supplied thousands of country papers with boiler-plate matter to fill their inside pages'. A knowledge of this is necessary to understand the statement: 'The ancients are discredited; Plato is boiler-plate' (O. Henry).   *Boom-stick* (1850–), a piece of heavy timber used in making a boom for impounding logs.   *Boot-leg* (1843–), the leg of a tall boot, sometimes used as a place for the concealed carrying of a flask of illicit liquor; hence *bootleg whisky, bootlegger* (1889), and *bootlegging*.   *Box*, in the sense of 'shaped like a box', as in *box-stove* (1820–), *box-sleigh* (1855), *box-sledge* (1884), *box-wagon* (1846–), *box-car* (1856–), *box freight-car* (1858), *box-cart* (1890–); *box-trap* (1840–), *box-stall* for horses and cattle (1885–), *box-house* (1881–), and *box-cañon* (1873–), a cañon with a flat bottom and vertical sides. Also, in other senses, *box-letter* (1832–), a letter to be placed in a private box at the post-office, *box-rent* (1841–), the rent paid for a post-office box, and *box-board* (1853–), board suitable for making boxes.   *Bread* in *bread-cask* (1778), *bread-grain* (1793), *bread-bowl* (1819–), *bread-board* (1869–), *bread-cake* (1876–), and especially *breadstuff* (1793–), in current use from the early years of the nineteenth century, and in the plural *breadstuffs* from 1831.   *Board* in many combinations where the usual English word would be 'wooden' or 'plank', as *board wall* (1698), *board partition* (1704), *board fence* (1718–), *board floor* (1836–), *board seat* (1852), *board shelf* (1859), *board walk* (1872–), *board sidewalk* (1883–). Other types occur in *board-log* (1647–), *board-pine* (1672–5), *board-yard* (1790–), *board-measure* (1809–), and *board-foot* (1896–).   *Bunk* in *bunk-room* (1855–), *bunk-house* (1876–), and *bunk-car* (1896–).   *Butt-cut* (1830–), the first portion of a tree cut off above the stump, familiarly used in various figurative senses, as 'he is the butt-cut of democracy'. *Butt-end* (1642–), the part of a tree-trunk immediately above the ground, is a specialized sense of the earlier English use.

In various other new combinations the first elements are of a less material nature. These include: *Bargain* in *bargain room* (1880), 'a place where remainders of lots are sold at smaller prices', *bargain counter* (1888–), *bargain day* (1898–), and *bargain sale* (1898–).   *Boom town* (1900–), a town originating in, or flourishing on account of, a boom in land or mining; 'as enthusiastic as the real estate agent in a boom town'.   *Bottom* in *bottom rock* (1864–), literal and figurative ('about the time I had reached bottom rock in my financial troubles'); *bottom dollar* (1866–), frequent in the phrase 'to bet one's bottom dollar'; and *bottom facts* (1877–).   *Bounty land* (1779–), land given as a bounty for military service, and *bounty lot* (1820–) in the same sense.   *Branch* in *branch bank* (1796–), *branch road* (1831–), frequently used of railways as well as roads, and *branch store* (1842–).   *Breakfast* in *breakfast horn* (1845–), used as a call to breakfast; *breakfast cap* (1863–), one worn at breakfast time; *breakfast tea* (1865–), often with the epithet 'English'; *breakfast station* (1872–), one on a stage-route where a stop is made for breakfast.   *Board bill* (1833–), the charges made, or the amount due, for board, as in 'the board bills are payable in advance'; *board book* (1872–), a book in which a member of the board of brokers recorded daily sales at the Exchange.   *Brand-book* (1665–), a book recording cattle-brands or marks.   *Bucket-shop* (1875–), a low-class liquor-shop; also (1881–), a dishonest brokerage establishment.   *Bulletin board* (1852–), one on which bulletins or other notices are posted.   *Burial lot* (1833–), a private plot in a cemetery; *burial case* (1851–) and *burial casket* (1866–), a coffin; *burial permit* (1888–), a certificate issued by the proper authorities granting permission to bury.

Verb-stems or verbal nouns appear in some combinations, e.g. *Bake-oven* (1777–), *bake-shop* (1789–), *bake-pan* (1790–; in English recorded from 1579 only), and *bake-kettle* (1846–).   *Break-back* (1856–9), a roof having the lower portion at a different slope from the upper. *Break-bone fever* (1862–), dengue fever, 'in which every bone in the body feels as if it were broken'. *Break-down* (1832–), 'a riotous dance, with which balls are often terminated in the country; a dance in the peculiar style of the negroes (Bartlett). *Buzz saw* (1860–), a circular saw. *Asking price* (1846–), the price asked, as distinguished from that which may be accepted. *Branding chute* (1893–), a narrow enclosure into which cattle are driven to be branded. *Breaking plough* (1853–), a heavy plough used in breaking up land, and *breaking team* (1839–), a team strong enough for this purpose. Also *breaking-up team* (1764–) and *plough* (1854).

Among new designations of persons are: *Axe-man* (1671–), a woodman (in early use also a fireman) working with an axe; 'then follow the axe-men, who clear away the bushes and fell the trees'. *Baggage agent*, &c. (see p. 233). *Bell-boy* (1879–), one who answers the bell in a hotel. *Bill-holder* (1846–), one who holds a bill or acceptance; the possessor of bills issued by a bank. *Bill-poster* (1809–), apparently American for the earlier English *bill-sticker* (1774). *Blanket Indian* (see p. 209). *Bone-picker* (1809–), among some Indian tribes, one who stripped the flesh from the bones of the dead. *Bootblack* (1817–), for the earlier English 'shoeblack'. *Bounty-broker* (1864), one who traded in the enlistment of soldiers during the Civil War. *Bounty-jumper* (1864–), one who obtains the bounty paid to recruits and then deserts, in origin also a Civil War term, along with *bounty-jumping* (1865–). *Brake-man* (1843–) on a railway train. The equivalent *brakesman* (1848–) appears at much the same date as in England. *Bunk-mate* (1877), one who shares a bunk with another.

Among the combinations with a personal designation as the first element are the following: *Baby* in the names of devices used in connexion with babies, as *baby-tender* (1845), *baby-jumper* (1847–), *baby-walker* (1856), *baby-wagon* (1853), and *baby-carriage* (1882–). Also *baby-show* (1867–), and *baby-act* (1873–) in the phrase 'to plead the baby-act', to set up a plea of legal infancy as a defence, 'pleading the baby-act of thoughtless irresponsibility'. *Bachelor's hall* (1828–), a house or establishment in which one or more bachelors live. *Band-wagon* (1855–), the wagon or ornamental car carrying a band, such as that of a circus, frequently in figurative use, as 'those Democrats who rushed into the Bryan band-wagon'. *Barber shop* (1832–), replacing the earlier *barber's shop* (1648–). *Blacksmith*

shop (1791–) and *blacksmith's shop* (1752–), the usual names
for a smithy.   *Butcher knife* (1822–), a large knife, now
applied chiefly to a kitchen utensil.

The number of adjectival collocations is very large,
without taking into account those already mentioned on
p. 203.   They include: *Adjunct professor* (1826–), a common title in American universities.   *Advanced standing*
(1790–), of a student in a university; *advanced student*
(1871–), and in a different sense, *advanced female* (1871–).
Almighty dollar (1836–), claimed by Washington Irving as
his invention.   *American system* (1824–), the policy of
fostering American industries by high tariffs and other
means. *American party* (1835–), a political party supporting American interests, especially one which was active
from 1853 to 1859, known also as 'the Know-nothing
party'.   *American plan* (1879–), the system of making
an inclusive charge for bed and board in a hotel, in contrast to the 'European plan' of charging for each separately.
Anxious bench (1832–) or *seat* (1835–), a seat near the
preacher in an evangelical service, on which those who are
strongly influenced by the preaching go or are taken to sit.
Such persons 'are called *anxious mourners*, and are led by
the ministers or deacons to the *anxious bench* or *seat* . . .
there to receive aid and comfort' (De Vere). Figurative
uses of *anxious seat* are common; 'Almira had long been
upon the anxious seat as regarded matrimony'.   *Astral
lamp* (c. 1830–), a lamp in which the descending light was
not interrupted by the reservoir; also called simply an
astral (1838).   *Back*, in a large number of terms denoting places or areas lying in the rear of the more settled
districts, as *back part* or *parts* (1698–), *backwoods* (1742–;
also *backwood* in attributive use, 1792–, and the adjective
backwoodsy, 1862–), *back country* (1755–), *back county*
(1755–), *back settlement* (1759–), *back swamp* (1772–), *back
town* (1822–). Similarly with names of persons living in
such places, as *back inhabitant* (1745–), *back settler* (1755–),
back farmer (1770–), *backwoodsman* (1784–), and *back
countryman* (1796–).   Other applications of *back* are
numerous, as in: *Back track* (1724–), one leading back to
the starting-point, frequently figurative, especially in the
phrase 'to take the back track'. *Back-trail* (1847–), in the
same sense. *Back-log* (1684–), a log, usually of large size,

set at the back of wood fire in a fireplace. *Back-stick* (1852–), a large stick placed above the back-log. *Back-fire* (1839–), a fire made to check an advancing prairie fire; also *back-firing* (1891–), the lighting of a fire for this purpose. *Back number* (1812–), an earlier number of a periodical or newspaper ('back numbers have been reprinted to supply Volume Nine'); frequent in figurative use from 1882, as 'Russia is a back number by several centuries'. *Back seat* (1829–), common in figurative use from 1859, especially in 'to take a back seat'. The adverbial sense of *back* appears in *back-action* (1845–), usually in attributive use, as 'a back-action machine'; *back-furrowing* (1855–), a method of ploughing by which two successive furrow-slices are laid towards each other; also *back-furrow* as a verb (1861–); *back-set* (1880–), to restore ploughed ridges to their original position by reploughing. From 'to talk back' comes *back-talk* (1884–); 'I never stood any back-talk from foremast hands'. *Bad lands* (1851–), stretches of barren and broken land in certain parts of the West. *Bad man* (1884–), in the West, a lawless character, a desperado. *Beaten biscuit* (1876–), a small hard biscuit, the dough for which is thoroughly beaten and frequently folded. *Best room* (1719), with *best parlour* (1771–) as a synonym, in common use to denote the best finished and best furnished room in a house, often reserved for special occasions. Similarly *best chamber* (1815–), the best bedroom. *Big*, in a large number of new expressions, e.g. *Big knife* (1750–), an Indian name for a Virginian or any American white man. *Big-horn* (1805–), the Rocky Mountain sheep. *Big head* (1805–), a bone disease in horses and cattle causing a swelling of the head; also (1820–) one or other fish having a large head, and (1850) conceit or egotism. *Big Muddy* (1825–), the Missouri River, and *Big Drink* (1846–), the Mississippi. *Big Pond* (1840–), the Atlantic. *Big Ditch* (1835–45), a contemptuous name for the Erie Canal. *Big road* (1818–), a main road or highway. *Big tree* (1860–), a sequoia tree of the Sierra Nevada. *Big bug* (1827–), *big gun* (1834–), and *big dog* (1845–), all sarcastic terms for a person of (real or fancied) great importance, one who 'goes the *big figure*' (1836–). *Big talk* (1837–), a conference or discussion with or among Indians; also (1860–) prolonged or 'tall' talk. *Big thing* (1875–), 'a very good prospect, a promising scheme', an undertaking likely to bring great results. *Big money* (1882–), a lot of money, large profits, high wages or salary. *Big four* (1886–), a combination of four important things, persons, or companies; specifically (1890–) the railway connecting the four cities of Cleveland, Cincinnati, Chicago, and St. Louis.   *Black*, in various collocations additional to those forming the specific names of plants, trees, animals, &c. (p. 203), as *black drink* (1772–), a decoction of the leaves of the yaupon, formerly used by the Indians of the southern states as a ceremonial drink and as a medicine. *Blackfeet* (1818–), an Indian tribe of the Western plains, with the singular *Blackfoot* (1837–). *Black code* (1840–), a legal code applying to the negro, especially in the southern states before emancipation. *Black law* or *laws* (1852–), a law or laws regulating the admission of negroes to a state or other area. *Black belt* (1875–), the portion of the South in which the negro population is densest; also (1883–), a belt of fertile black land in certain states, as Alabama and Mississippi.   *Blank book* (1712–), a book of clean writing paper; 'a paper with printed questions and a blank book were placed before each candidate'.   *Blind staggers* (1833–), the staggers in sheep or other animals. *Blind bridle* (1833–), a bridle fitted with blinds or blinkers. *Blind tiger* (1883–) and *pig* (1887–), a place where illicit liquor is sold; from the latter comes also *blind-pigger* (1894–), one who keeps a 'blind pig'. *Blind baggage-car* (1901–), one that has no door in the end next the engine.   *Bloody Ground* (1777–), Kentucky, more fully called the 'dark and bloody ground'. *Bloody shirt* (1875–), the symbol of continued hostility, or of the desire to provoke it, between opposing parties, originally between the South and North after the Civil War, frequent in the phrase 'waving the bloody shirt'. A thoroughly American sentence from 1888 is: 'I can easily fancy what a cry would have been raised. The waving of the bloody shirt would not have been a marker' (i.e. would have been nothing to it). *Bloody chasm* (1876–), the estrangement between the South and North caused by the Civil War. *Blue* in many names of trees, plants, animals, &c. (p. 203), and in various other collocations. *Blue laws* (1781–), 'those rigorous judicial regulations and proceedings which form

a part of the early history of the colony of Connecticut',
later also applied to similar regulations at other times and
places. *Blue-skin* (1782), an ardent supporter of the Revolution; also (1787–), a person of puritanical morals,
a Presbyterian (1821–47), a negro (1863–6), a federal
soldier, &c. *Blue-belly* (1827–57), an American or Yankee,
in the latter sense also *blue-bellied Yankee* (1857–); in
later use (1866–), a soldier in blue army uniform, originally a Southern nickname for one of the 'boys in blue',
i.e. the Northern or Federal troops. *Blue-nose* (1830–),
a native of New Brunswick or Nova Scotia; also (*c.* 1840–)
a variety of blue-skinned potato, and (1883) a species of
clam. *Blue lights* (1813–), the lights reported to have been
shown at New London in Connecticut as a signal to the
British fleet during the war of 1812–15; hence applied to
persons suspected of disloyalty, also attributively as *blue-
light men* (1817–), *federalists*, &c. *Blue streak* (1830–), a
streak caused by rapid movement of light; also (1842) a rapid
rush, and (1847–), a continuous stream of words, frequent
in 'to talk a blue streak'. *Blue Point oyster* (1805–), a small
oyster from the beds off Blue Point on Long Island, or
one similar to this, also called simply *blue point* (1880–)
and *blue-pointer* (1844–). *Blue hens' chickens* (1840–),
soldiers of the state of Delaware, which from these is
called the *Blue Hen* (1840) or *Blue Hen State* (1867–).
Blue Monday (1869–), a Monday regarded as depressing or
trying by reaction from unusual indulgence or exertion on
the previous day; 'by this name clergymen designate the
day. . . . But Blue Monday does not belong exclusively to
clergymen.'   *Boiled dinner* (1805–), a dinner of which
the main course consists of meat and vegetables boiled together. *Boiled shirt* (1861–) or frequently *biled shirt* (1851–),
a white or dress shirt.   *Broad alley* (1731–) and *broad
aisle* (1807–), the main aisle or passage-way in a church,
'the outsiders would enter, and make their way through
the broad and side aisles'. *Broad hoe* (1672–), a hoe having
a blade about a foot wide, used in the cultivation of corn,
cotton, tobacco, &c. *Broadhorn* (1819–), a species of flat
boat formerly used on rivers, especially the Ohio and
Mississippi, 'an immense oar is placed on the roof on each
side near the bow (which has given these boats the nickname of "broad horns")'; also (1847–), the big horn or

Rocky Mountain sheep, and (1900) a long-horn ox. *Brown stone* (1836–), a brown sandstone extensively used as a building material, frequent in attributive use (1860–), especially in *brownstone front* (1866–). As this stone became 'an almost proverbial synonym for all that is desirable and elegant', the epithet came to mean 'pertaining to the well-to-do class', as in 'the brownstone members of that institution', 'the brownstone vote, as it is called'.

Of combinations with an adjective as the second element, two may be noted. *Appearing* with a qualifying adjective preceding it, as *best-appearing* (1839–), *fine-appearing* (1857–), *new-appearing, rude-appearing*, &c.   *Bridle-wise* (1840–), 'applied to a horse which is guided by pressure of the bridle against his neck instead of by pulling on the bit' (Cent. Dict.); hence *bridle-wisdom* (1895).

The prefix *ante-* is used to form the attributive phrases *ante-bellum* (1870–) and *ante-war* (1878–) to designate the period before the Civil War or anything connected with that time, as *ante-bellum times, days, style, ante-war money*, &c. *Ante-revolutionary* is recorded earlier in American use (1837–) than in English (1860) and may have actual precedence in date.   *Anti-* has been profusely employed in forming such combinations as *anti-federalist* (1787–), *anti-fogmatic* (1789–), *anti-democrat* (1802–), *anti-union* (1813), *anti-slavery* (1820–), &c. In the new dictionary no fewer than seventy of these are given as clearly of American origin.

III

Although a considerable body of words has been added to American English by adoption from other languages native to, or brought into, the American continent (especially the various Indian tongues, Dutch, French, and Spanish), the number of these in ordinary use is really small in comparison with the vocabulary as a whole. Much more numerous, and frequently more important, are those new words which are independent of such origins, and have arisen either as natural developments from the normal sources of English or to all appearance are bold innovations in the realm of speech. Some examples of these two classes are given in the following lists.

Aborigines had been used by English writers from the

seventeenth century onwards in reference to other races than those of ancient Italy, and in America the name was naturally given to the Indian inhabitants of the continent from at least 1724, although Webster disapproved of it as late as 1828, with the remark, 'not an English word. It may be well to let it pass into disuse.' It came, however, to be so familiar as to assume the colloquial forms *abrogoines* (1830) and *abbregynes* (1837). The greater need for the designation in America makes it natural that the adjective *aboriginal* appears in 1698 ('the aboriginal natives of America') and the noun ('the want of fire-arms among the American aboriginals') before 1752, whereas the earliest dates for these in the English record are 1788 and 1845 respectively.   The purely Latin *admittatur* was the name given at Harvard from 1683, and later also at Yale, to the certificate of admission given to a student by the president and other members of the faculty.   The French *affiant* for the person making an affidavit appears in common use from 1807, 'the deputy marshal denied affiant the right to make a bond'.   *Alumnus* (1696–) has been a much more familiar term in American colleges and universities than in British, both in the singular and plural, and in attributive uses as *alumnus orator, alumni society, alumni meetings*, &c. Distinctively American is the feminine *alumna* (1882–), with the plural *alumnæ*, and attributive uses as *alumna teacher*.   The *ambrotype* (1857–), a photograph on glass in which the dark background shows through, was an American invention.   *Anæsthesia* and the adjective *anæsthetic* were introduced by O. Wendell Holmes in 1846; as a noun the latter appears in 1854.   *Appendicitis* was suggested by Fitz in 1886 as preferable to 'peritonitis'. The French *automobile* appears a little earlier in American than in British use, and the noun with its derivatives *automobilism, automobilist, automobilize* ('it is scarcely an exaggeration to say that Paris is becoming automobilized'), its abbreviation *auto*, and its compounds, as *autobus, autocar, autocycle*, have in the main had an American currency.

The colloquial type includes a considerable number of distinctive and often expressive words, not a few of which have sooner or later been accepted as current English. Such are: *Ad* (1868–) as an abbreviation of 'advertisement', first in vogue 'in the newspaper offices and the advertising business'.   *Aide* (1777–) and *aid* (1780–) as abbreviations of 'aide-de-camp'.   *Bach* (1855–) as an abbreviation of 'bachelor', frequent in 'an old bach'. Also *bach*, v. (1878–), to live as a bachelor, to keep house without woman's help; 'the men don't like "baching", as it is called in the wilds'. *Bee* (1769–), a gathering of neighbours and friends to accomplish some task in common, especially by way of assisting one of the number: 'the cellar of our new house was dug by a *bee* in a single day'. The purpose of the meeting is often expressed by a defining term, as *husking*, *logging*, *quilting bee*. A *bee* is also a combined presentation of gifts to a minister by members of the congregation (1823–).   *Belittle*, first used by Jefferson (1781–2) in the sense of making small, reducing in size ('the tendency of Nature to belittle her productions on this side the Atlantic'); subsequently (1797–), to speak slightingly of, to disparage.   *Biz* (1862–), a common colloquial abbreviation of 'business'.   *Blaze* (1750–), to mark a tree by slicing off a piece of bark (cf. p. 208); also (1750–) to mark or indicate a path by making blazes on the trees, and figuratively (1850–) to mark out a course of action for others to follow; 'pioneers who blazed the way to future conquest'.   *Blizzard*, first recorded (1829–) in the senses of a violent blow or a volley of shot, and (1835–) a crushing retort, remark, or speech. The modern sense of a violent storm of fine driving snow accompanied by intense cold appears first in a local newspaper of Estherville, Iowa, for April 23, 1870, and rapidly attained general currency after that date.   *Bloomer*, in *bloomer costume*, *dress*, *trousers*, &c., and the plural *bloomers*, date from 1851, the name being taken from that of Mrs. Amelia Bloomer of Seneca Falls, N.Y., who, however, merely edited the magazine in which the new costume was first described. 'She did not invent it, was not the first to wear it, and protested against its being called by her name', says Thornton. The derivative *bloomerism* appears in the same year.   The verb *bluff*, as a term in the game of poker, or in its general sense (frequently with 'off') first appears in 1839, the noun in 1845; also *bluff game* (1845–), *bluffer* (1850–), and *bluffing* (1850–).   *Bogus* (1827–), originally an apparatus for making counterfeit coins (also *bogus press* or *machine*); then (1839–), money made on a bogus, counterfeit coin or

notes, and current in attributive use from 1842, at first
with *money*, afterwards (1857–) in general use.   *Boodle*
(1833–) in the phrase 'the whole boodle', the whole lot;
also (1858–), counterfeit money, money obtained dis-
honestly, money in general, and more recently (1884–),
money used as a means of political bribery or as party
spoils.   *Boost* as a verb (1815–), to raise or lift, to push
or shove up, frequent in figurative contexts from 1835; as
a noun (1825–), a push that assists one to rise, assistance
towards attaining success or reputation. Both verb and
noun have long had wide currency.   *Boss* (1806–), sufficiently Americanized to obscure its Dutch origin (*baas*),
used attributively from 1836 ('boss shoemaker', 'boss poli-
ticianer', 'boss loafer', &c.) and acquiring its political sense
by 1875; 'the custom which makes "bosses" of men who
control election gangs'. Hence the verb *boss* (1856–) and
the derivatives *bossism* (1851–), *boss-ship* (1882–), and *boss-
dom* (1888–).   *Bowery* (1788–), a large shelter or building erected to accommodate those attending a gathering or
meeting; 'a handsome grove, through the middle of which
runs a long frame bowery'.   *Bowie knife* (1836–), named
after Col. James Bowie, though the invention of it was
claimed by his brother, Rezin P. Bowie; also common in
the abbreviation *bowie* (*a.* 1846), 'the real bowie is from
nine to ten inches long, with one edge'. Different de-
scriptions of it are, however, given at different dates.
Brag (1838–), as an adjective (no doubt derived from the
noun or verb) in the sense of 'fine, excellent, first-rate'.
Bread (1797–), as a verb in the sense of supplying with
bread; 'what corn I have will scarcely bread the negroes
and feed the work-horses'.   *Brogan* (1835–), a stout
coarse shoe, one of a small number of Irish Gaelic words
adopted in the language.   *Brother Jonathan* (1780–), the
typical New Englander or Yankee, or the representative of
the American people as a whole. There is no proof that
by this any particular person was originally intended; the
statement that it became current through Washington
using it of Jonathan Trumbull is late and unsupported by
evidence.   *Buck* as a noun in a number of senses, of
which the chief are the poker term in 'to pass the buck'
(1872–), frequently used figuratively for shifting responsi-
bility to another, and the act of bucking on the part of

a horse (1884–). Also *buck* as a verb in several distinctly American senses, viz. to display disinclination or resistance (1851–), frequently with 'against' (1859–); to drive or rush into, to force one's way, &c. (1861–); to truss up a person by way of punishment (1853–); to throw away money in gambling (1851–), and *to buck the tiger*, to play against the bank at monte or faro.   *Buckboard*, originally (1839), 'a stout, springy plank laid upon the bolsters of a wagon'; latterly (1869–) a very light four-wheeled vehicle.   *Bummer* (1856–), an idler, loafer, or sponger; also (1861–) a Civil War soldier who left the ranks and went raiding on his own account; (1869–) an adventurer on the Stock Exchange, and (1872–) a political hanger-on, of no real service to his party.   *Bunco* (1872–), a swindle perpetrated by such means as card-sharping, a sham lottery, &c. Hence *bunco* (1875–) as a verb, to swindle, and *bunco-steerer* (1875–), a swindler.   *Bunkum* (1828–) and *buncombe* (1846–), originating in the phrase 'talking to (or for) Buncombe', the constituency in North Carolina represented by a speaker in Congress, who persisted in going on with his speech in spite of the inattention of his audience. As an adjective a different *bunkum* occurs (1848–) in the sense of 'fine, excellent, first-rate'; 'some of our moons are bunkum—first rate, as is everything American'.

IV

Survivals of older English uses account for a certain number of what are now regarded as distinctive Americanisms. Some of these may fairly be reckoned as examples of the growth of the language, since they have obtained far wider currency and have come into greater prominence in their new home than they ever did in their old. To that extent they are real additions to the ordinary vocabulary.

The following examples of these survivals and expansions occur under the letters A and B. Where no remark is made as to the downward American limit, it may be assumed that the usage has continued down to the past half-century or to the present day.

A with verbal substantives in an active sense, current in literary English from the sixteenth to the eighteenth century, survives latterly only as an archaism (especially in the Biblical 'to go a-fishing') or in dialect use. It has remained more generally current in American colloquial and occasionally literary use, and affords an indication of national pursuits in such instances as *a-fowling* (1622–), *a-fishing* (1624–), *a-hunting* (1624–), *a-whaling* (1675–), *a-gunning* (1700–), *a-husking* (1737–), and *a-sleighing* (1764–). Other incidental examples are *a-scalping* (1757), *a-scouting* (1760), *a-wooding* (1832), *a-chopping* (1846), *a-logging* (1871), *a-lumbering* (1871), *a-huckleberrying* (1854), and *a-moose-hunting* (1858).   *Admire* as an intransitive verb in the sense of 'to be desirous or pleased, to like' followed by an infinitive, recorded in English from a short period in the seventeenth century (1645–76) and now current only in dialect, has survived colloquially in spite of the purists: 'my comrade said he did not admire to smell a whale, and I adopt his sentiments while I scorn his language', Mark Twain wrote in 1864.   *Appraisement*, the act of valuing a property or estate, recorded in English from 1642 to 1745, has remained in regular use; 'the classification and appraisement of such lands' occurs in a statute of 1913.   *Approbate*, to approve or sanction formally or legally, after 1600 only in Scots law, continued in American use to at least 1847, and survived still later in the general sense of approving or regarding with favour; 'in no single instance does Holy Writ approbate it'.   *Arrearages*, arrears of payment or of pay, of which the English record closes in 1691, is fully evidenced from 1631 to 1881; in that year a newspaper informs its subscribers 'No paper discontinued until all arrearages are paid'.   *Bank-bill*, a bank-note, current in English between 1696 and 1809, can be cited a little earlier (1682) in American use, and has all along remained current beside *bank-note* (1714–).   *Bed-chamber*, archaic or formal in nineteenth-century English, remained later in natural American use (to 1864 at least).   *Bed-cord*, a stout cord passing from side to side of a bed to support the mattress, recorded as English only *a.* 1625–1720, was in common American use down to the close of the nineteenth century.   *Beef*, a single animal of the ox-kind, obsolescent in English since the eighteenth century, is still in regular use, formerly with the plural *beefs* as well as *beeves*.   *Beets*, the plural of *beet*, has not been displaced by *beet-root* as in English, where it did not survive

the eighteenth century.   The Irish *bonnyclabber*, known
to English writers for about a century from 1631, has remained in full use in various parts of the United States.
Bottom, a stretch of low-lying land beside a river, an allu-
vial hollow, apparently only a dialect term in England
after the early years of the eighteenth century, has remained one of the distinctive topographical terms. Beside
some of the larger rivers there are first, second, and third
bottoms, and without the article it is used as the equivalent of *bottom-land* (p. 236).   For *bowling alley* the
English record closes in 1703; the American begins in
1825 and continues to the present time.   *Bowling green*
is common to both countries, but *bowling saloon* is purely
American.   *Browse*, the small shoots or twigs of trees
and shrubs on which cattle and horses feed, appears in
English use down to 1837; in America, beginning with
1721, it can be abundantly illustrated all through the
nineteenth century.   *Brush*, in the two senses of brushwood, has similarly remained in full use, while in English
it appears to have been discontinued about 1820–30. This
survival accounts for the introduction of the verb *brush*
(1730–) in several senses.   *Buggy*, current in English
from 1773 to 1866 or later, has now become distinctively
American, and has also acquired the new senses of the
kitchen-car of a freight-train, a small trolley, and a sliding
board used in bridge-work. Attributive uses, all purely
American, are also numerous, as *buggy harness, horse,
plough, sleigh, wagon, whip*.   *Bull-beef*, slightly represented in English from 1572 to 1785, occurs in New
England in 1635, and has been common in the nineteenth
century: 'New Yorkers do not look on bull-beef and ham
as luxuries'.   *Buzzard* in the phrase 'between hawk and
buzzard' is recorded in English only in 1636 and 1662;
the American examples range from 1832 to 1904. As con-
temptuously applied to a person, the English evidence ends
with 1822; the American covers the period 1807–1909,
and the instances show a natural colloquial use of the
word: 'I ain't never heard of the buzzard himself since
that day'.

This survey, by no means exhaustive, of the vocabulary
covered by the first two letters in the Dictionary of American

English affords ample evidence of the extent to which the language has been enriched without the adoption of extraneous elements and of the various causes and conditions which have contributed to this. The remarkable number and variety of the additions in this small portion of the alphabet are some indication of the task which lies before the scholar who undertakes to write a real 'History of the English Language in America', or, if he prefers it, of 'The American Language', on the basis of the dated and documented material which the dictionary will ultimately contain, together with such additions as may still be made to it.

V

In the earlier portion of this study (pp. 200–3) it was pointed out that it is frequently doubtful, on the available evidence, whether a particular use or phrase can safely be set down as an Americanism, since the absence of any English record in the existing dictionaries is not conclusive proof against English currency, and an apparent American priority in date may be misleading. In a number of instances the doubt can be settled by direct research in sources likely to yield the evidence desired; this is especially the case with scientific and technical terms. In others the finding of the evidence is a matter of chance, and depends to a great extent on the fact that the problem has presented itself and has drawn attention to what might otherwise have been readily overlooked.

Two or three examples will sufficiently illustrate this. The *building trades* are recognized in American sources from 1890 onwards. In the O.E.D. *building trade* is mentioned, but not illustrated, in a part of the work published in 1888. It might actually have been cited from Swift's verses on Vanbrugh's House, 'On earth the God of wealth was made Sole patron of the building trade'. This, however, does not help towards establishing the date at which the phrase, either in the singular or the plural, became a fixed collocation as it is at the present day, or towards deciding whether it came simultaneously into general use in Britain and America.

An apparent Americanism is thus commented on by De Vere: "The great importance which a crop of grass has for all stock-raisers and the Indians ... has led to the use of the peculiar phrase in which the youth, who is no longer a boy and not yet a man, is picturesquely said to be *between grass and hay*'. This application of the phrase is recorded from 1848, and a different use of it in 1891. An American origin is, however, eliminated by its occurrence in 1744 in the *Modern Husbandman* of William Ellis (III. i. 78): 'April and September are reckoned the worst months to make butter in, because then the season is between grass and hay'.

Although *pan* in the sense of a hard substratum of soil has been in English use from 1790 (or even from 1630), the collocation *hard pan* appeared to be so exclusively American, that in the O.E.D. it was characterized as 'U.S.' and in the D.A.E. was unquestioningly accepted as an Americanism, with the earliest example of the date *a.* 1817. But in a 'General View of the Agriculture of the County of Kincardine', by James Donaldson, published in 1796, there occurs the passage: 'Neither does wood of any description thrive where there is a hard pan of concreted matter below the first spade depth'. The phrase is thus one of those which have become American by usage, though not so in origin.

The extent to which doubtful cases remain in the first three letters of the alphabet will appear from the following lists, in which the earliest American date is given, as it appears in the D.A.E., and is followed by the corresponding English date whenever this can be ascertained.

Acclimated, 1800 : 1856
Acclimation, 1826 : 1859
Address (to the king, &c.), 1660: 1751
Addressee, 1810 : *a*1858
Admiralty court, *a*1649
Advisory, *a.*, 1787 : 1862
Agriculturalist, 1805–9 : 1819
Alarm clock, 1751
Alarm gun, 1761
All-overish, *a.*, 1833 : 1851
Annunciator (the instrument), 1853 : 1879
Apple pudding, *c*1788 : 1807
Apple sauce, 1801 : 1824
Armed neutrality, 1780 : *c*1803

Artificer (military), 1758 : 1804
Assortment, 1736 : 1791

Back-handed (fig.), 1800 : 1865
Back porch, 1840
Back road, 1788
Back room, 1788
Back seat, 1829
Back shed, 1789
Back street, 1638
Baking powder, 1857
Bank account, 1799
Bank check, 1801
Bank messenger, 1850
Bank parlor, 1881
Bank runner, 1851

Bank vault, 1842
Bar iron, 1653 : 1677
Bean soup, 1837
Bell-buoy, 1838
Bell-hanger, 1789
Benefit society, 1811 : 1845
Benevolent society, 1811
Berth (situation), 1745 : 1788
  ,,   (on a ship), 1771 : 1809
  ,,   (in a room), 1805-9 : 1885
Berth-deck, 1814
Black frost, 1709
Black Maria, 1847 : 1874
Block out, v. (= design), 1753 : 1837
Blowing up, 1822 : 1874
Blow-out (a spree), 1834 : 1856
Boat-building, 1780 : 1863
Boatload, 1680
Bog-hole, 1839
Bond-holder, 1838 : 1865
Bondsman, 1713 : 1754
Book muslin, 1759 : 1836
Box iron, 1666 : 1746
Brain-fag, 1851
Branch pilot, 1783 : 1864
Brass band, 1837 : 1861
Breakfast table, 1775 : 1838
Breeches maker, 1727 : 1831
Brevet (military), 1776 : 1811
Bring down the house, 1865
Broad-brim (person), 1774 : 1797
Broad-brim (hat), 1834 : 1855
Brickyard, 1731 : 1864
Broke, a. (penniless), 1821 : 1851
Brood mare, 1821 : 1878
Bullet pouch, 1757
Burglar alarm, 1840 : 1884
Burglar proof, 1856 : 1882
Burial ground, 1775 : 1803

Cabin bell, 1702
Cabin door, 1824
Cabinet minister, 1806
Cabman, 1840 : 1850
Calf-pen, 1667 : 1856
Call loan, a1859 : 1882
Camp fire, 1675 : 1837
Camping ground, 1837 : 1867
Camp kettle, 1755 : 1805

Canal boat, 1818 : 1843
Canalling, 1813 : 1834
Canal lock, 1844
Cane-back chair, 1778
Cane-bottomed, 1841 : 1877
Cane-seat (chair), 1851
Cane-seated, 1869 : 1881
Cap'n (= captain), 1829 : 1880 dial.
Cap-sheaf, 1782 : 1846 dial.
Carding machine, 1788 : 1830
Carding mill, 1816
Card rack, 1790 : 1826
Care-free, a., 1854 : 1919
Carpenter's rule, 1815
Carpet factory, 1834
Carpet-weaver, 1827
Carriage body, 1812
Carriage-maker, 1819
Cart-box, 1688
Cart-bridge, 1633
Cartridge belt, 1874
Cartridge paper, 1678 : 1712
Cartridge shell, 1868
Cart-road, 1700 : 1868
Casemate, v., 1717
Cash-box, 1855 : 1864
Cash boy, a1872
Cash girl, 1880
Cashiership, 1820 : 1884
Casting (= article cast), 1788 : 1851
Casting net, 1644 : a1680
Casting vote, 1671 : 1692
Castor hat, 1655 : 1680
Catch basin, 1874
Catch bolt, 1858
Cattle-fair, 1819
Cattle-shed, 1845
Cattle show, 1815 : 1851
Caul fat, 1799 : 1882
Causeway, v., 1702 : 1740
Cavalry boot, 1867
Cave (in), v., 1707 : 1830 dial.
Cede, v. (territory), 1784 : 1798
Ceded, ppl. a., 1803 : 1844
Census taker, 1840
Centre (= central), c. 1703:1791
Centre table, 1833 : 1868
Centurial, 1817 : 1877
Chain bridge, 1809 : 1818

Chain gang, 1835 : 1858
Chair-back, 1880
Chair factory, 1827
Chair-maker, 1684 : 1813
Chaise-house, 1746 : 1812
Chaise-maker, 1759
Chamber-mate, 1766 : 1886
Channel pump, 1758
Channel shoe, 1762
Channel-way, 1833
Chap-book, 1798 : 1824
Charcoal-burner, 1825 : 1841
Check-rein, 1849
Cheese-cloth, 1657 : 1741
Cheese-maker, 1868
Cheese-making, 1831 : 1846
Cheque-book, 1817 : 1848
Cherry-brandy, 1686 : 1728
Cherry-wood, 1821
Chewing tobacco, 1792
Chicken hawk, 1827 : 1890 *dial.*
Chimney-back, 1698 : 1764
China closet, 1771 : 1807
China trade, 1788
Chin-music, 1836 : 1877 *dial.*
Chip hat, 1759 : 1771
Chipper, *a.*, 1838 : 1875 *dial.*
Chipper, *v.*, 1712 : 1825 *dial.*
Chirpy, *a.*, 1837 : 1859
Chocolate cake, 1876
Chocolate cream, 1865
Chocolate-grinder, 1725
Chocolate mill, 1785
Christmas gift, 1826
Chuck-hole, 1847
Chunky, *a.*, 1751 : 1856 *dial.*
Churn-dasher, 1845
Cigar-box, 1846
Cigar-case, 1846
Circular, *n.*, 1789 : 1818
Circular saw, 1817 : 1825
Circus rider, 1839 : 1876
City court, 1786
City directory, 1815
City editor, 1870
City fathers, 1853
Civil rights, 1721
Clay-bank, 1839
Clearance, 1727 : 1755
Click-beetle, 1861 : 1881
Climbing rose, 1836

Clog dance, 1869 : 1881
Clog-dancer, 1873
Close, *a.* (of a contest), 1828 : 1855
Close carriage, 1845
Clothes-bag, 1834 : 1879
Clothes-closet, 1825
Clothes-horse, 1775 : 1806
Clothes-pin, 1852
Clothes-pole, 1865
Clover field, 1848
Clover hay, 1748
Clover seed, 1723
Coach lace, 1805
Coach office, 1818 : 1833
Coach-painter, 1814
Coach-trimmer, 1840
Coal-boat, 1818
Coal-breaker, 1871
Coal-bunker, 1840
Coal-cart, 1839
Coal company, 1852
Coaling station, 1853 : 1870
Coal-stove, 1834
Coal-train, 1861
Coal-yard, 1805
Coastwise, *a.*, 1817 : 1885
Coating, 1768 : 1802
Cobweb muslin, 1807
Codfishery, 1735 : 1753
Codfishing, 1637 : 1734
Cod-hook, 1634
Cod-line, 1634 : 1794
Cold frame, 1857
Cold wave, 1884
College-bred, 1842
College course, 1818
College dues, 1670
College education, 1771
College hall, 1643
College library, 1693
College life, 1836
Colonial, *a.*, 1776 : 1796
Colonizer, 1781 : 1817
Coming out, 1850
Commandant general, 1803:1827
Complimentary ticket, 1874
Concert room, 1774 : 1799
Congestive, *a.*, 1834 : 1864
Congregationalism, 1716 : 1835
Conner (= cunner), 1685 : 1836

Conscript, *v.*, 1813 : 1887
Constitutionality, 1787 : 1801
Consular, *a.*, 1789 : 1830
Continental, *n.*, 1777 : 1828
Contra-dance, 1803 : 1830
Copper mine, 1637
Copper ore, 1713
Copying press, 1785 : 1820
Corner cupboard, 1813 : 1838
Cotton;card, 1775
Cotton goods, 1792
Cotton-growing, 1868
Cotton market, 1840
Cotton-seed, 1774 : 1795
Cotton-spinning, 1827 : 1843
Council room, 1809
Country doctor, 1865
Country road, 1862
Country trade, 1863
County bridge, 1668 : 1809
County jail, 1699 : 1794
County rate, 1665 : 1807

County town, 1670 : 1711
Coupon bond, 1861
Court-room, 1677 : 1766
Court-time, 1646
Cow-bell, 1652 : 1869
Cow-common, 1639
Cow-keeper, 1640 : 1680
Cow-keeping, 1652 : 1883
Cow-shed, 1835 : 1865
Cow-yard, 1637 : 1798
Cradler, 1766 : 1835
Crate, *v.*, 1871
Crockery crate, 1849
Cross-section, 1835 : 1870
Cross street, 1661 : 1827
Cross walk, 1808
Cupola furnace, 1837 : 1845
Curling tongs, 1763 : 1846
Currant bush, 1724 : 1791
Custard-cup, 1825
Cut glass, 1819 : 1845
Cut-grass, 1817 : 1849